Brothers & Sisters

Number Nineteen
CAROLYN AND ERNEST FAY SERIES
IN ANALYTICAL PSYCHOLOGY

David H. Rosen, General Editor

The Carolyn and Ernest Fay edited book series, based initially on the annual Fay Lecture Series in Analytical Psychology, was established to further the ideas of C. G. Jung among students, faculty, therapists, and other citizens and to enhance scholarly activities related to analytical psychology. The Book Series and Lecture Series address topics of importance to the individual and to society. Both series were generously endowed by Carolyn Grant Fay, the founding president of the C. G. Jung Educational Center in Houston, Texas. The series are in part a memorial to her late husband, Ernest Bel Fay. Carolyn Fay has planted a Jungian tree carrying both her name and that of her late husband, which will bear fruitful ideas and stimulate creative works from this time forward. Texas A&M University and all those who come into contact with the growing Fay Jungian tree are extremely grateful to Carolyn Grant Fay for what she has done. The holder of the McMillan Professorship in Analytical Psychology at Texas A&M functions as the general editor of the Fay Book Series.

A list of titles in this series appears at the end of the book.

Brothers & Sisters

MYTH AND REALITY

Henry Abramovitch

Foreword by David H. Rosen

Texas A&M University Press • College Station

Manufactured in the United States of America

This paper meets the requirements of ANSI/NISO Z39.48-1992

(Permanence of Paper).

Binding materials have been chosen for durability.

LIBRARY OF CONGRESS CATALOGING-IN-PUBLICATION DATA

Abramovitch, Henry, 1950– author.

Brothers and sisters : myth and reality / Henry Abramovitch ; foreword by David
H. Rosen. — First edition.

pages cm. — (Carolyn and Ernest Fay series in analytical psychology; number
nineteen)Includes bibliographical references and index.

ISBN 978-1-62349-190-1 (cloth: alk. paper) —

ISBN 978-1-62349-218-2 (ebook)

1. Brothers and sisters—Psychological aspects. 2. Developmental psychology.
3. Brothers and sisters—Family relationships. 4. Brothers and sisters—
Religious aspects. I. Title. II. Series: Carolyn and Ernest Fay series
in analytical psychology ; no. 19.

BF723.S43A37 2014

155.44'3—dc23

2014009224

To my brother and sister,

who together taught me

what it means to be a brother,

what it means to have a sister.

To sisters and brothers everywhere.

Contents

Series Editor's Foreword

DAVID H. ROSEN

Brothers and Sisters is an important and timely volume. I first met the author in 1990 at a conference on "The Archetype of the Healer" organized by Anthony Stevens and held at Oxford University. At that time I felt an immediate, brotherly bond with Henry, so it is gratifying for this book to come to the Fay Series, which I have edited.

The sister-and-brother relationship is fundamental to our global community. I put the female first here because that's where we all originated.[1] And for the survival of our increasingly complicated world, love for our brothers and sisters is the right way and the way of justice. Henry Abramovitch offers a true understanding of the depth and breadth of this topic. He even includes the erotic or taboo in love and marriage in a historic revelation of the fact of royal incest—in Egypt, Peru, and Hawaii—and draws special inspiration from the siblings stories in scripture, from Cain and Abel through to the sisters and brothers who are the children of Job.

The book made me think more deeply about my own sister and brother. I come from a family of five children: three girls and two boys. We liked and loved each other as sisters and brothers are inclined to do. I have one older and two younger sisters and a younger brother. Despite sibling rivalry, which can lead to conflict and even death (as Cain and Abel taught us), our relationship taught us to get beyond divisiveness. Like brothers and sisters in a nuclear family, the world family must transcend war and establish peace in our difficult and beautiful civilization.

Perhaps it is synchronicity that Texas A&M University is developing a "Peace Campus" in Nazareth, the Arab capital of Israel. Nazareth is home to Christians, Muslims, and Jews. A peace initiative such as this educational one could be a vital seed that grows and prospers there. It is a dream that may allow for peace in the Holy Land, and on earth, when we all will be our brothers' (and sisters') keepers.

In this insightful volume, Abramovitch puts us in touch with our own experience of both actual and archetypal siblings to help us understand the power and the danger of this human relationship. In my own family, which started with love between my mother, Barbara (a non-Jew), and my father, Max (an Orthodox Jew), my mother converted because my father's parents would not attend the wedding unless she did. However, my parents decided to develop a Unitarian fellowship as an amalgamation of all religions, and that is how we were brought up. This upbringing yielded a Baptist (my oldest sister), a spiritual but unaffiliated individual (me), a Protestant (my brother), a Hindu (my younger sister), and a Unitarian (my youngest sister). We all concluded that there is a God, a sacred wholeness of humanity and ethics, and "Nature" (as in Spinoza's philosophy).

This text explores, in depth, the myth and reality of brothers and sisters in a variety of religions and cultures. Drawing on linguistic nuances and cultural expectations, it also provides both a provocative consideration of the absence of siblings from the lives of great theorists of depth psychology and a helpful discussion of clinical practices related to brother-sister dynamics. It provides a new vocabulary for discussing sibling transference and countertransference.

Brothers and sisters. What could be more crucial in this time of divisiveness, conflict, and war? If we can embrace our sisters and brothers, familial and otherwise, it is possible that we will transcend disintegration and hatred and proceed down a path of integration, love, and union.

If we become a world of united nations and move toward a whole-world community as one family, there is hope for our troubled civilization. This book is written by a wandering Jew who grew up in Montreal, Canada, studied at Yale, trained in Israel, and lives in Jerusalem. It contributes to that better union of all our brothers and sisters. Once we are aware (as we are), the choice is ours to make.

I pray that it is for love and justice, the harmony of one human family, and the long life of our planet earth.

David H. Rosen
Eugene, Oregon
General Editor, Carolyn and Ernest Fay
Series in Analytical Psychology

Preface

I love to tell jokes. I find great pleasure making people laugh, in creating, if only for a moment, a community of laughter. So it was natural for me to search for a joke about brothers and sisters for these Fay lectures. I searched and searched, but I could not find one. Apparently the subject of sisters and of brothers is not funny. On the other hand, the archetypal experience of being a brother, or having a sister, promises so much: loyalty, togetherness, a lifelong unbreakable bond. There can be something so easy between us and those with whom we shared a womb or a bedroom. Your sister and brother probably know you better than any other person. They saw what went on offstage, behind closed doors; they shared the smells of childhood; they will stand by you, side by side, through separations and celebrations, through divorce, mourning, marriage, and more. You and they go through life together—or at least that is the way it is supposed to be. That is the promise of the myth of sisterhood and brotherhood. Often, however, sibling reality is very different.

As I was giving the Fay Lectures, many people from the audience came up to me during the breaks. They told me their sibling stories. With tears sliding down their cheeks they spoke of a brother who had cut off all contact, a sister who had stolen an inheritance, and other sister and brother wounds. These wounds are often invisible. We cannot determine people's sibling status just by looking at them. Often a sibling identity is a closed door of secret joys and/or suffering. My goal is to open that door.

Ultimately I did remember a joke. It was one I had heard from my own mother, herself with a complex sibling history. It was a Talmudic joke about a theoretical sister, at the intersection of Jewishness and siblingness. Here it is:

A sickly young Rabbinical student was about to go on his first, and probably last, date before his arranged marriage. He was terrified. He had never before been alone with a female. He sought the advice of his Rabbi, asking, "What will I say to her?" The Rabbi reassured and guided him, "First, speak of family. Then about love. And finally, conclude with philosophy." The student responded: "Okay. First family, then love, and finally philosophy."

When he was ushered into the room, he encountered a similarly terrified young woman who had never been alone with a man. The Rabbinical student began boldly with "family": "Do you have a sister?" he asked. She answered meekly, "No." Noticing a bowl of oranges on the table, he asked, "Do you like oranges?" Again she responded softly, "No." Two topics were gone. Only philosophy remained. With a look of inspiration, he asked, "And if you had a sister, do you think she would like oranges?"

This joke about a theoretical sister taught me something that will be no surprise for a Jungian. It is that imaginary siblings, sisters we meet in dreams and brothers in fantasy, are no less important than our actual siblings.[1] We all carry within us the image of the ideal brother and the perfect sister, and of their evil twins. Much of our lives as sisters and brothers is played out in the gap between the myth of the ideal sibling and the often painful reality. This book tries to explore that gap.

We have difficulty talking about siblings in part because we suffer from a poverty of words to express the experience of being a sister or brother. In English the standard term for brothers and sisters, "siblings," is problematic in terms of feelings: it is not only gender-neutral but also experience-distant and emotionally flat. No one says, "I would like to introduce you to my sibling." Rather, we say, "I would like to introduce you to my sister/brother." In short, speakers of the English language have difficulty speaking intimately of siblings. However, not every language shares this peculiar emotional distance. In Swedish the word for sibling, *syskon*, carries a warm, emotional connotation. That is the sense in which I will use "sibling:" the intimate togetherness that brothers and sisters are meant to be.

English is also rather restrictive in defining who is a sister or brother, sharply distinguishing full brothers and sisters from half-sibs, step-sibs, and all forms of cousin. Most cultures are more generous and inclusive in who is a brother or sister. Among the Iroquois of the Eastern Woodlands of Canada and the United States, all parallel cousins (mother's sister's children and father's brother's children) are called "brother" and "sister." In traditional Hawaiian culture, all first cousins on both sides are called "brother" and sister." The Hebrew term *akhim,* which will most concern us in this study, has a creative ambiguity unknown to English speakers. It can equally mean "exclusively brothers," "brothers and sisters together," "close kinsmen," or even "brother-men." It contrasts only with terms for "exclusively sisters." A hint of this semantic ambiguity can be seen when Abraham twice calls his wife "sister"[2] even though she is certainly his wife. Sarah likely was a close female relative on his father's side designated "sister" (or in technical language, a patrilineal "classificatory" sister) as in the Iroquois and Hawaiian patterns. In the Middle East, biologically unrelated persons who nurse at the same breast are called "milk brothers" and "milk sisters." They share incest taboos and special intimacy. Nonbiological brotherhood and sisterhood (such as in religious orders) and "blood" brotherhood (in which one chooses to be a "sister" or a "brother") provide an intense sense of loyalty and togetherness. Fertility treatments have created another whole potential range of siblings. For example a surrogate mother may give birth to two children, who share no genetic material but might be called "birth siblings." Those with a father's semen in common might be termed "semen siblings" or, with a shared female egg, "ovum siblings."

The English terms "sister" and "brother" make no reference to birth order. One may specify birth status—"older sister" or "youngest brother"—but to do so is not obligatory. In many cultures, by contrast, sibling hierarchy is so ingrained in the cultural psyche that there is no birth-order-neutral term for a sister or a brother. One must always specify birth status. In the South Indian language Tamil, for example, one must specify whether one is referring to an older brother (*anna*) or a younger (*tambi*) or to an older sister (*akka*) or younger (*tangai*). The language has no birth-order-neutral kinship terms.

Many languages have a special kinship term for the eldest child, as does biblical Hebrew: *bekhor* and *bekhora* are for eldest son and eldest daughter respectively. Biblical Hebrew even has a special ritual name for a first-born child: *petakh rekhem* ("womb opener"), for whom the ritual "redeeming of the firstborn" is performed. If a woman had a prior miscarriage, stillbirth, or pregnancy of any sort, the *bekhor* (eldest son) will not necessarily be the womb opener.

In many cultures, eldest children, especially eldest sons, have special rights and obligations. In Yiddish, for example, the eldest son is often called "my *kaddish*." *Kaddish* refers here to the ritual obligation of the eldest son to recite the kaddish, the prayer over the dead, at the grave and for the rest of the mourning year. His birth status imposes a defining religious duty that is at the core of his family identity. A few languages even have a special word for "youngest child," such as *hakatan* in biblical Hebrew and *mezinke* in Yiddish. There are societies in which the youngest son inherits the family flocks. Such kinship systems emphasize how birth-order hierarchy is fundamental to what it means to be a sister or a brother. In this book I try to create the beginnings of a new vocabulary for talking about siblings.

In the following pages I make extensive use of the Hebrew Bible to illuminate the complex sibling situation. To evoke a sense of biblical Hebrew, I draw on a contemporary translation by the American-Jewish biblical scholar Everett Fox. His version, I believe, gives the best feel for the original Hebrew. The Fox translation is modeled on the pioneering German translation of the Bible by Martin Buber and Franz Rosenzweig, which strives "to echo the Hebrew, and to lead the reader back to the sound structure and form of the original."[3] The resulting version is faithful, comprehensible, and poetic. It is refreshingly balanced between loyalty to the Hebrew text and accessibility to the reader. Fox's version, nevertheless, has a few peculiarities. The four-letter personal name of the biblical God, the tetragrammaton, traditionally pronounced "adonai" ("my Lord" or "the Lord") is left an enigmatic "YHWH." Fox also gives the Hebrew version of names and then their meaning. For example, here is Fox's Rachel explaining the naming of her long-desired son, Yosef (Joseph):

God has removed / asaf
my reproach!
So she called his name: Yosef,
saying:
May YHWH add / Joseph
another son to me!
(30:23–24)

To preserve familiar English versions of biblical names, I use Fox's explanations but not his unfamiliar transliterations: "Cain" instead of "Kayin," "Abel" instead of the more-accurate "Hevel." I also draw on translations, as indicated, such as JB (Jerusalem Bible), JPS (Tanakh, Jewish Publication Society), RA (Robert Alter), and KJ (King James). Unless otherwise indicated, chapter and verse numbers refer to Genesis.

Every book tells a story but is itself also a story. This book begins and ends anchored in my relationships with my own brother and sister. I feel blessed in having both a brother, Lavy, and a sister, Ilana. Each relationship is unique, but I benefited enormously from knowing what it is to have one sibling of each gender. Each has taught me so much about what it means to be a brother and a sister. I cannot imagine my life without them. They are among those rare siblings who become truly a brother, truly a sister. I shall describe my relationship with each of them in the very personal afterword. This book is dedicated to them.

Chapter 1 deals with the remarkable neglect of siblings in depth psychology and the impact of the founders' birth order on their personalities and theories. Chapter 2 provides an overview of both the mythology and the archetype of brothers and sisters. Chaper 3 describes the ideal brothers of two Indian epics. Chapter 4 gives a close reading of the primal scene in the life of siblings via the story of the first brothers, Cain and Abel. Chapter 5 shows that the rest of the sibling stories in Genesis provide a series of psychological strategies in response to the primal scene. Chapter 6 looks at the unusual sibling situation of Moses and Job. Shifting to the clinical dimension, chaper 7 employs active imagination to explore clinical examples of sibling transference and countertransference, the inner and outer roles of brothers and sisters in the practice of healing.

I was honored and delighted to travel to Texas A&M University to give the Fay Lectures. I want to thank all those who made the lectures possible, but especially David Rosen, friend and "mensch," a truly decent human being who invited me, nurtured me, and traveled from Oregon to be my host. It was a pleasure to thank others who made my visit to College Station so special: Frank McMillan, Carolyn Fay, Paul Wellman, former President Loftin, Taha Jangda, Mary Lenn Dixon, and Thom Lemmons.

I also want to thank my Fay Lectures predecessors and friends, who set an archetypally high standard but provided key information that smoothed my way: John Beebe, Murray Stein, Astrid Burg, Jan Wiener, Beverly Zabriske, and Ann Ulanov. I would also like to thank Susan Pollard, Renos Papadopoulos, Ludwig Betak, Micky Weingarten, Murray Shugar, Mary Harsany, Fortuna Cohen, and Ann Shearer.

In addition, I want to thank Everett Fox for his unique modern translation of the Five Books of Moses.

I wish to express special thanks to three Jungian colleagues who shared their own material on sisters and brothers and who read and commented on the manuscript: Kristina Schellinski (who shared her important work on "replacement children"), Helen Brammer-Savlov (who shared her excellent unpublished thesis on the topic of siblings), and Lisbeth von Benedek (whose insightful work has appeared in French).

I am grateful to those who read drafts of the manuscript, who enriched this work, especially my sister and brother. In the past twenty-five years I have given many lectures, seminars, and workshops on brother/sister dynamics in different parts of the world: the C. G. Jung Club of Montreal, Canada; "Jews for the Nineties," Stockholm, Sweden; the Guild of Pastoral Psychology, London, England; the C. G. Jung Institute, Switzerland; the Bitter Lemon Group, Jerusalem, Israel; the C. G. Jung Society of Calgary, Canada; the Ontario Association of Jungian Analysts, Toronto, Canada; the Irish Association of Analytical Psychology, Dublin, Ireland; Kehilat Mevakshei Derech, Jerusalem, Israel; the Czech Developing Group, Prague, Czech Republic;

the Johannesburg Developing Group, South Africa, the Jung Societies both of Sydney, Australia, and of Western Australia; and an extended version at the South African Association of Jungian Analysts, Capetown, South Africa. I gave clinical seminars on working with siblings to social workers at Talbiyeh Center for Mental Health, Jerusalem. I also gave the terminal presentation to the Israel Association of Analytical Psychology before it split into three.[4] I want to thank all those who participated in these events, in which we were able to learn in depth from each other about what it means to be sisters or brothers. Thanks also to friends, colleagues, patients, and strangers for sharing sibling stories and sibling insights.

Special thanks to my dear friend David Dean Shulman, Professor of Indian Languages and Literature, Hebrew University, Jerusalem, who guided in the world of all things Indian; my brotherhood of "study partners" (*chavruta*), with whom I learn together week after week; George Savran, Professor of Bible, Schechter Institute of Jewish Studies, Jerusalem, who kindly kept me informed of recent developments in biblical scholarship; Jonathan Price, Professor of Classics and Ancient History, Tel Aviv University, who also made illuminating suggestions; Shlomo Naeh, Professor of Talmud, Hebrew and Jewish Thought, Hebrew University and member of the Academy of the Hebrew Language; Eliezer Schwartz, fellow Professor at Tel Aviv Medical School and Founding Director of the Center for Geographic Medicine and Tropical Diseases; Rabbi James "Jim" Ponet, Howard M. Holtzmann Jewish Hillel Chaplain at Yale University, who showed me that even Job had siblings. Author and critic Ioram Melcer twice recovered inadvertently deleted drafts from the depths of my computer. Rosalie Siegel shared her sibling stories and encouraged the work in its early stages. I would also like to express deep gratitude to key mentors who made an enormous difference in my own life: Arthur Candib, my headmaster at Herzliah High School, Montreal; Fred Oscanyan, Leonard W. Doob, William McGuire, Daniel Levinson, and Robert Jay Lifton at Yale University; and my analysts, Ray Walker and William Alex of blessed memory.

My three children, Ella, Tamara, and Hillel, allowed me an intimate parent-centered perspective on sibling relations; and I thank them for

giving me permission to write about them. Finally, there are no words
to express my thanks to my wife, Iva Bader Abramovitch, who was my
first reader and "helpmate," who taught me what it means to grow up
without brothers or sisters.

Henry Abramovitch
Jerusalem, 2013

Abbreviations

The following abbreviations represent biblical translations used in this text:

JB *The Jerusalem Bible: Reader's Edition.* Edited by Alexander Jones (Garden City, NY: Doubleday, 1968).

JPS *JPS Hebrew-English Tanakh* (Philadelphia: Jewish Publication Society, 2001).

KJ *The Bible: Authorized King James Version* (Oxford: Oxford University Press, 2008).

MF Michael Fishbane, *Text and Texture: Close Readings of Selected Biblical Texts* (New York: Schocken Books, 1979).

RA Robert Alter, *The Five Books of Moses: A Translation with Commentary* (New York: W.W. Norton, 2004).

SM Steven Mitchell, *Genesis: A New Translation of the Classical Biblical Stories* (New York: HarperCollins, 1996).

Passages not citing a translation are from Everett Fox, trans., *The Five Books of Moses: Genesis, Exodus, Leviticus, Numbers, Deuteronomy,* vol. 1 of *The Schocken Bible* (New York: Schocken Books, 2000).

Brothers & Sisters

Prelude

ACTIVE IMAGINATION 1

I want to begin with an active imagination.

Imagine the sister or brother you would most like to have. . . .

Now think about the brother or sister with whom you have the most complex relationship. . . .

Much of what I will say in this book lies in that painful space between your ideal sibling and your real ones, between the myth and the reality.

CHAPTER 1

The Neglect of Sisters and Brothers in Depth Psychology

There is, it is said, no Jewish Oedipus.
Robert A. Paul, *Moses and Civilization*, 11.

A sibling is forever. . . .
Elisa Albert, *Freud's Blind Spot*, 76.

Siblings more than parents, more than teachers, and
   friends and lovers and pets shape "the people we are."
Elisa Albert, *Freud's Blind Spot*, 1.

I have often wondered what might have happened had Jung and Freud used the Bible instead of Greek mythology for their inspiration. Greek mythology is full of intense conflict between parents and children, such as Chronos swallowing his children, Oedipus killing the father who had abandoned him as a child, and Demeter decimating nature in mad mourning for her kidnapped daughter. In contrast, the Bible, especially Genesis, has few such intergenerational conflicts.[1] Instead, the major emotional dynamics are between sisters and among brothers, a topic virtually absent from Greek mythology. The greatest Greek heroes, such as Odysseus and Oedipus, were solo children.

Given that brothers and sisters are so fundamental to human experience, their neglect in depth psychology is truly surprising.[2] I suspect that one of the most important reasons for the neglect of siblings in Western societies is the expectation of early sibling separation. Charles Nuckolls, an anthropologist who studied village culture in South India, wrote: "Siblings in a Euro-American context are culturally expected to leave home and separate for life. Important decisions about economics and social life are expected to be made along with one's parents, spouse, friends, or work associates, but not primarily with one's siblings."[3] He reported that Western indifference to sibling relationships is nothing less than extraordinary to his Indian informants. South Asian villagers frequently inquire about the siblings of their visitors and typically express shock when confronted with answers like "I don't know," or "I haven't seen my brother/sister for years."[4] China, with its one-child policy, is the first society to deliberately seek to create a world of "little Emperors" without brothers or sisters.[5] I wonder if the growing selfishness in China is a byproduct of children growing up without siblings. I suspect that a true depth psychology of brothers and sisters will emerge, not from the sibling-deprived West, but from the sibling-centered developing world.

Growing up, we typically spend more time with our brothers and sisters than with our parents, and our relationship with our siblings usually lasts longer. In an age of divorce, mobility, and alienation, the sibling bond is often the only one that really lasts.[6] Siblings and birth order appear to play a crucial order in the success of a marriage and friendship patterns.[7] A positive relation with a sibling is one of the key indicators of successful aging and longevity.[8] The persistent, positive role of siblings as attachment figures and transitional objects is supported by research that shows how siblings function to protect each other, especially early and later in life. Think how Hansel and Gretel provide each other a profound sense of security when they are lost in the forest and how they work together to kill the "witch" and find their way home. Significantly, children with siblings adjust far better than singletons following a divorce. Brothers and sisters often serve as secure attachment figures. As the actress Katherine Hepburn wrote:

> I cannot say anything in detail about my sisters and brothers. They are so much a part of me that I simply know that I could not have been me without them. They are my "box"—my protection.[9]

Yet she herself was scarred forever. When going up to the attic to look for some forgotten treasure, she found her beloved brother hanging, dead, from the rafters. In her family it was something never talked about.

Brotherhoods and sisterhoods provide some of the most powerful collective human experiences. They are at the heart of the rallying cry of the great ideologies of inclusion: "The Brotherhood of Man," "Liberté, Egalité, Fraternité," "Sisterhood is powerful!" When we want to evoke a connection with a stranger, we automatically use the language of brotherhood/sisterhood, as in the famous Depression-era song, "Brother, Can You Spare a Dime?" Nuns and nurses call each other "sister." Brotherhoods and sisterhoods, whether religious or secular, provide a profound sense of identity, belonging, and togetherness. The greatest compliment one can give a friend is to say, "You are like a sister (brother) to me." How many of us can say that about our own flesh and blood?

A Birth-Order Bias

The stark avoidance of sibling dynamics in depth psychology, I believe, is directly related to the birth-order bias of Freud and Jung. Their role as favored eldest child may have influenced psychodynamic theory itself. Prophecy Coles wrote, "Psychoanalytical theory seems to have colluded with the wish to be the only child."[10] Freud's theory of the "family romance" is very much the story of a firstborn child in a most nuclear of families. Some of the most famous clinical case studies of children, such as Freud's "Little Hans,"[11] Virginia Axline's "Dibs: In Search of Self,"[12] and, as we shall see, Donald Winnicott's "The Piggle,"[13] are actually case studies in the psychology of the firstborn child.

The sibling experience of the founders of depth psychology may well have led them to disregard unconsciously the importance of brothers and sisters. Both Freud and Jung, successful, secure eldest children, were relatively unconcerned with either their own siblings or sibling issues in general. Their theories reflect their birth-order bias. Freud, the beloved firstborn of his mother, wrote, "A man who has been the indisputable favorite of his mother, keeps for life the feeling of being a conqueror, that confidence of success which often induces real success."[14] He did have many brothers and sisters, but the "First Freud" received very special treatment. He was the only child to have his own room and lamp. When he complained that his sister's piano playing distracted him from his studies, his mother had the piano removed. Not surprisingly, he interpreted the dream image of rodents as the intrusive presence of unwanted younger siblings.[15]

As a very young child, Sigmund was greatly influenced by the birth and sudden death of his infant brother Julius. Julius was born when his older brother was seventeen months and died five months later.[16] This brief sibling relationship likely played a formative role in the development of Freud's psychoanalytic theories. Writing to a confidant, Freud confessed: "I welcomed . . . my younger brother (who died within a few months) with ill wishes and real infantile jealousies. . . . His death left the germ of guilt in me."[17] His lifelong concern with feelings of guilt may have its origins in his own feeling of guilt as a sibling survivor.[18] Strangely, Freud ignored the importance of being a sibling survivor in some of his best-known case histories, such as "Dora" and the "Wolfman." In his autobiography the Wolfman claimed that his depression was triggered, not by a primal scene, the traumatic experience of witnessing his parents making love (as Freud had argued), but by the suicide of his sister, whom he considered his "only companion."

Jung, by contrast, was an only child for his first nine years, until his sister Johanna Gertrud, called "Trudi," was born. She never did play much of an active role in his life: "At bottom she was always a stranger to me, but I had great respect for her."[19] Jung's experience seems typical of siblings born more than seven or eight years apart, which might represent the psychological limit of sibling kinship libido. Siblings growing up too far apart do not go through developmental phases together, nor do they share core emotional experiences. They often grow up as "sibling-strangers." Jung and his sister did have strongly polarized identities. Writing in his autobiography, Jung notes: "My sister, [had] a delicate and rather sickly nature, in every respect different from me. . . . I was rather emotional, whereas she was always composed, though very sensitive deep down."[20]

Nonetheless, Jung, like Freud, did have a strong emotional reaction to the birth of his sister, an experience for which he was totally unprepared:

> My father brought me to my mother's bedside, and when she held out a little creature that looked dreadfully disappointing: a red, shrunken face like an old man's, the eyes closed, and probably as blind as a young puppy, I thought. On its back the thing had a few single long red hairs which were shown to me—had it been intended for a monkey? I was shocked and did not know what to feel. . . . The sudden appearance of my sister left me with a vague sense of distrust.

The birth of a younger sibling raised feelings in Jung that he may never have understood fully.[21] "As though born to live the life of a spinster,"[22] she never married but lived with their mother. Unmarried sisters often are fated to look after aging parents. When she died following an apparently harmless operation, he "was deeply impressed" to discover that "she had put all her affairs in order beforehand, down to the last detail."[23] Jung's relationship with his own sister may well have contributed to his understanding concerning the nature of different psychological types.

No Room in the Theory for Anyone Else

Siblings also are neglected in depth psychology as a result of the increasing importance of the Great Mother and particularly of the mother-infant interaction. Starting with Jung, psychoanalytic theory turned away from Freud's concern with the Father and the Oedipal triangle and gave increasing emphasis to the Mother. This trend was furthered by the important contributions of Ronald Fairbairn, Melanie Klein, Donald W. Winnicott, Erich Neumann, Michael Fordham, Thomas Ogden, and many others. Each emphasized that early mother-infant interaction was *the* critical phase for psychological development. Within their theoretical formulations, whether the "facilitating environment" (Winnicott), "maternal symbiosis" (Mahler), "Great Mother" (Neumann), or "de-integration process" (Fordham); a sense of "Basic Trust versus Mistrust" (Erikson); or schizoid (Fairbairn), paranoid and depressive (Klein), or "autistic-continguous" (Ogden) positions, there simply is no place for siblings. Lacking representation in psychic reality, siblings were psychologically absent, at least in theory.

Theories serve not only as models of the workings of the psyche but also as maps that point out what is important to notice: what is essential and what is incidental, what is signal and what is noise. Even the best theory has an unconscious bias that excludes data outside its framework. In the absence of a theory to guide us, we do not attend to what we are not trained to find. As a result, case histories regularly fail to report sibling status altogether. In my clinical work I am surprised how often patients tell of previous therapies avoiding sibling conflict. A middle-aged woman explained: "I wanted to talk to my analyst about a problem I had with my brother. But he insisted that the real issue was my sexual fantasies about my parents."[24] Another woman told me that the one time she consulted a therapist, "We *never* discussed my being a twin or my problematic relationship with this twin and yet . . . being a twin has had an impact on all the other relationships in my life and is the *central* point to explore in working out any unresolved conflicts."[25] I wonder whether these examples are the result of neglect or countertransference bias or whether the analysts have worked on their own sibling wounds.

In *The Primitive Edge of Experience,* Thomas Ogden presented a clinical illustration of a twenty-three-year-old female graduate student whose brother, she felt, was like "just another tenant in the boarding house."[26] And she related to Ogden in a similar fashion. Yet, surprisingly, he never conceptualized her lack of emotional connection to him in terms of sibling transference. Moreover he confessed that he often forgot that she had a brother. Imagine an analyst forgetting that the patient had a mother! When therapists do note birth order or sibling dynamics, they lack theory that specifies how brothers and sisters might play a role in the life of the psyche.

A case in point is Donald Winnicott's famous account of his treatment of a little girl, Gabrielle, known as "the Piggle." This account deals with the emotional shock of a toddler at the birth of a younger sister. After more than a year and a half of treatment, the mother wrote to Winnicott and revealed: "My anxieties were very intense at the time of [the sister] Susan's birth—I forgot whether I told you that I have a brother, whom I greatly resented, who was born when I was exactly the same age as Gabrielle was when Susan was born."[27] Winnicott had neglected to ask the mother if she had any siblings, although it is now widely thought that parents may unconsciously recapitulate with their children their own troubled sibling experience. Winnicott makes no comment on the mother's dramatic revelation, nor does the revelation influence her treatment. Winnicott is widely regarded as one of the most seminal thinkers, but he seems to have had no way of thinking about siblings, even when the Piggle insisted on being called by her younger sister's name. In retrospect, it seems likely that Susan played the role of the Piggle's "shadow sibling." A shadow sibling receives the projection of all that is unwanted or unacceptable in oneself and is both envied and hated for having those very qualities. A shadow sibling is, therefore, the opposite of the ideal sibling, a compensatory negative and unconscious figure. When shadow figures are not differentiated from real siblings, the shadow figures may exert an intense but hidden impact on relations with the siblings. Winnicott did note elsewhere how the birth of a younger sibling may provide an older child with an opportunity to learn that, in time, sibling hatred can be transformed into sibling love—and that the parents still love each other. This may well be true, but note that Winnicott conceptualizes sibling experience exclusively from the firstborn perspective. This turning of hatred to love seems certainly true of the Piggle, whose mother wrote toward the end of treatment:

Gabrielle is very close to Susan, handles her with great circum-
spection, cajoles her, is often the mediator between her and
us. We are struck by how often she will try and get her way by
deflecting Susan's attention or by some inventiveness, rather
than by direct attack, though sometimes she is miserably, and
helplessly consumed by jealousy, and Susan can do nothing
right. The other day, in the middle of a fierce fight, she suddenly kissed Susan and said: "But I like you." This is very different
from Susan, who alternately looks up to Gabrielle fervently
and ruthlessly wants to destroy her superiority.[28]

Research suggests that Gabrielle's experience is rather typical: initial
frustration (usually expressed toward the mother, less often toward
the baby) is transformed gradually into lasting companionship.[29]

Melanie Klein, a major psychoanalytic theorist who also influenced Jungian thought, especially in the London School, was reputed
to be somewhat dogmatic. A rather nasty joke highlights this unat-
tractive quality. Two candidates in London are traveling to their training analysts when the tube [subway] breaks down. The first candidate
says, "Oh, no! I'm going to be late. My analyst, a classical Freudian,
will interpret it as resistance. I'll say it was the tube; he won't agree;.
The whole session, the whole analysis, will be destroyed at this very
moment." The other candidate says, "I'm not worried. I'm going to a
Kleinian. She'll just start without me."

Missed sibling dynamics pervade Melanie Klein's most famous
case studies: Gunther and Franz (1926),[30] Erna (1932),[31] and Richard
of *Narrative of a Child Analysis* (London: Hogarth Press, 1975). Juliet
Mitchell, a scholar of Klein's, work concludes, "Melanie Klein's work
is a fascinating instance of the repression of siblings from observa-
tion and theory."[32] Unconscious sibling dynamics might also lie at the
heart of Klein's work: she was the youngest of four children. Klein's
biographer, Phyllis Grosskurth, quotes her as saying, "I was very
keen to get some attention and to be more important than the older
ones."[33] Klein viewed envy, which lies at the heart of her theory, as innate, arising spontaneously in the infant from birth in response to the
maternal breast. Grosskurth, however, suggests that envy embodied

her own experience as a powerless baby sister. Later as an adult, she claims, Klein envied her sister, Emilie, "for seeming to have the fulfilled emotional life that she herself craved, as well as—in the face of all her troubles—a certain serenity."[34] On the other hand, Klein had an exceptionally close relationship with her brother, Emmanuel, whom she called "the best friend I ever had." Grosskurth concludes: "Brother and sister were twin souls, sharing the same sorts of moods and reactions. He was her surrogate father, close companion, phantom-lover—and no one was able to replace him."[35] This idealized relationship may have been complicated further by Emmanuel's death when Klein, at age twenty-one, was on the verge of adulthood and married life. The impact of this relationship, I suspect, may be found in her view that childhood sexual relations between children, especially brothers and sisters, often have "a favourable influence upon the child's object relations and capacity to love."[36] I wonder whether Klein's unconscious feelings toward her own siblings played a hidden, but significant, role in her theory, as they did in her life.

As a cultural fantasy, a profound sense of intimacy comes from combining origin and eros in the body of a single, familiar person. Mythology from all over the world describes enduring examples of sister-brother marriages. The best known are Zeus and Hera in Greek mythology, Isis and Osiris in Egyptian mythology, Izanami and Izanagi in Japanese tradition, and Fuxi and Nuwa in China. Jean Cocteau's literary classic, *Enfants Terribles* (New York: Brewer & Warren, 1930) presents an innocent incident of childhood incest that ends badly. The archetypal image of brother/sister-lover is central to ancient Egyptian love poetry: "I have found my brother in his bed. My heart is glad beyond all measure; The mouth of my sister is a rosebud. Her breast is a perfume."[37] The biblical Song of Songs gives poetic expression to this unique intimacy when the "sister" says: "Ah, why are you not my brother, nursed at my mother's breast!" (Song 8:1, JB) and her "brother" replies, "My sister, my promised bride, you ravish my heart. " (Song 4:9, JB) These poignant poems express symbolic yearning for an "inner marriage" with the ideal sibling.

Perhaps the most profound tradition concerns the very first brother-sister pair, Adam and Eve. In most English versions of the Bible,

Adam is mistranslated as "man" when he might better be referred to as "human" (as Fox does), part of an untranslatable, poetic sequence: *dam/adam/adama,* blood/human/earth. Adam is created before Eve, who then is constructed from his *tzela.* The Hebrew word *tzela,* usually translated as "rib," may equally mean "side." In fact the word appears thirty-nine times in the Hebrew Bible and most often it clearly means "side." If we follow this Hebrew tradition,[38] reading Adam's *tzela* as "side," then Adam was not male. Rather, he was an androgynous Siamese twin, in which male and female halves were joined side by side. This interpretation resolves the apparent contradiction in the second story of creation. Genesis 5:1–2 clearly states, "Male and female He created them." This image of an undivided, primordial state reflects Jungian views of the psyche as holding within the primal unity both the feminine and the masculine before the division of consciousness into opposites. God's fateful surgery separated the male and female halves. As a result, Adam and Eve, twin brother and sister, are able to turn around, emerge from the shadow, and see each other face to face for the first time. The tension between known and unknown as the seedbed of love is movingly expressed in Adam's cry of recognition: "This-time, she-is-it! Bone from my bones, flesh from my flesh." (2:23) This powerful tradition clearly implies that the natural state of humankind is one of brother and sister becoming husband and wife.

Moving from mythology to reality, actual brother-sister incest is everywhere forbidden except in the royal courts of three early civilizations: ancient Egypt, the Inca of Peru, and the island kingdom of Hawaii.[39] In each court a divine brother married his royal sister. This sibling incest uniquely assured the purity of their regal lineage and the divinity of their child, the next ruler. Such permissible royal incest may illuminate the terrible story of two of King David's children, his eldest son, the crown prince Ammon, and his beautiful half-sister, Tamar. Infatuated with the unattainable Tamar, Ammon suffers from "love sickness," saying, "I am in love with Tamar, the sister of my brother Absalom." (2 Sam. 13:4, JPS) On the advice of his cousin, Amnon hatches a plot to lure Tamar into his bedchamber. He pretends to be sick and begs his father, David, to send his favorite sister,

Tamar, to prepare special foods to restore his health. David orders her to do so. While she is feeding him, he grabs her and begins to rape her. Resisting her brother's brutal advances, she says: "Don't, brother. Don't force me. Such things are not done in Israel. Don't do such a vile thing! Where will I carry my shame? And you, you will be like any of the scoundrels in Israel!" Instead she goes on to propose an incestuous royal marriage: "Please, speak to the king; he will not refuse me to you." (2 Sam. 13:12–13, JPS) Tamar's strange plea clearly implies that their father would sanction such a sister-brother marriage (as in nearby Egypt). Amnon refuses to listen and rapes her. His passion, once sated, turns to loathing, and he throws her out despite her protest, "Please don't commit this wrong; to send me away would be even worse than the first wrong you committed against me." (2 Sam. 13:16, JPS) Scripture describes the bitter aftereffects of this sibling sexual-abuse trauma: "Tamar put dust on her head and rent her ornamented tunic she was wearing; she put her hands on her head [a gesture of wild grief; cf. Jer. 2:37] and walked away, screaming loudly as she went." (2 Sam. 13:19, JPS) Forlorn, Tamar takes refuge in the house of her full brother Absalom, who asks her to join the family conspiracy of silence: "For the present sister, keep quiet about it; he is your brother. Don't brood on this matter." (2 Sam. 13:20, JPS) When Tamar's father, King David, learns of the rape, he is greatly upset but does nothing. One ancient tradition[40] claimed that David did not rebuke Amnon because he was the favored first-born. Absalom waits two years and then has Amnon killed in revenge for the wrong done to his sister. Tamar is not mentioned again in the narrative, and we never learn the rest of her story.[41] One can only imagine how she felt without her father's support and having been silenced by her brother. I assume that she never recovered, neither marrying nor bearing children. Absalom subsequently had three sons and a daughter. The sons are unnamed, but the beautiful daughter is named Tamar. (2 Sam. 14:27) If Absalom followed the Jewish Ashkenazi practice of naming children for dead relatives, Tamar probably died young.

Tamar's experience reflects contemporary research and my own clinical experience. The fantasy of erotic intimacy between sisters and brothers might be archetypally enticing, but the effects of actual brother-sister incest are overwhelmingly negative.[42]

> *When an inner situation is not made conscious, it*
> *appears outside as fate.*
> C. G. Jung, *Aion: Researches into the Phenomonology*
> *of the Self,* para 126.

Jung on Brothers and Sisters

Jung did understand the psychological importance of brother and sister archetypes. In *Answer to Job,* he wrote: "Yahweh had one good son and the one who was a failure. Both Cain and Abel and Jacob and Esau correspond to this prototype, as does the motif of the hostile brothers in all ages and all parts of the world. Innumerable modern variants cause dissension in modern families and keep the psychotherapist busy."[43]

Emma Jung gave two lectures on "the brother motif" to the Psychology Club in Zurich that, sadly, have been lost.[44] Jungian psychology takes much of its inspiration from mythology and fairy tales, in which sibling stories and tensions abound. For example, in Grimm's fairy tales, the youngest son, who at first appears to be the despised simpleton, emerges as the victorious hero 92 percent of the time.[45] He is interpreted symbolically as representing the undervalued, inferior aspect of the personality. Edward Edinger, author of *The Bible and the Psyche: Individuation Symbolism in the Old Testament,* wrote that the twins Jacob and Esau represent the division within the psyche between "ego and shadow and ego and Self."[46] Siblings in dreams and fantasy were likewise understood as symbols of different parts of the personality, typically anima, animus, or the shadow. Mario Jacoby discussed the distinction between an outer and an inner sister in connection with a dream.[47] John Beebe, who gave the second Fay Lecture, *Integrity in Depth,* writes elsewhere about his archetypal sibling counter-transference as a "transference brother, a fellow sufferer enjoying a respite from the arduousness of adulthood, and a model for the animus that will relate to some creative aspect of her personhood

. . . experiencing the Self . . . [as] an 'organ of acceptance.'"⁴⁸ Jung and post-Jungians understood the mythic power behind the archetypes of sister and of brother. But what lies at the core of being a sister and having a brother? What is at the heart of the archetypal experience of sisters and brothers?

CHAPTER 2

The Sibling Archetype

*Virtually every biological system featuring close
contact among close genetic relatives surely
contains a shifting equilibrium between incentives
for selfishness and those for altruism.*
Mock and Parker, *The Evolution of Sibling Rivalry*,
411.

Cooperation-Competition Continuum

As both a psychologist and an anthropologist I am often struck by the contrast between how these disciplines relate to brothers and sisters. Psychology, especially depth psychology, emphasizes conscious and unconscious conflict in terms of "sibling rivalry," "dethronement," or even the displacement of marital conflict in what has been called "Oedipal sibling triangles." On the other hand, in anthropology, siblings are viewed much more positively as the main social glue by which societies are held together. In many places the union of brothers and sisters is the main metaphor for how society operates. Universally brothers and sisters, no matter how much they may fight among themselves, will unite to fend off an external threat, as expressed in the well-known Arabic proverb, "I against my brother, my brother and I against my cousin, my cousin, brother, and I against the world."

Jung taught that every archetype has two contrasting poles. The Great Mother is both the all-loving and all-nurturing Earth Mother and the devouring, destructive, regressive Dragon: Mother Mary and

Medusa. Likewise we may think about the brother/sister archetype as having opposing poles. At the negative pole are rivalry, hatred, and murderous rage arising from a struggle for dominance and hierarchy, as illustrated in the stories of Romulus and Remus, Seth and Osiris, and the three sisters in Shakespeare's *King Lear* and in many of Grimm's fairy tales. Even before Medea killed her children, she murdered her brother to assure Jason's success. Evolutionary biologists have discovered how common siblicide is and the conditions under which it is to be expected: "When available resources are insufficient (or likely to be so) for all concurrent offspring to survive, sibling rivalry is expected to become fatal."[1] In the animal kingdom, the murderous aggressiveness of siblings is illustrated when a female hyena kills its twin sister to qualify as leader of a pack.

In a comparable fratricide, recorded in Judges 9, Abimelech massacred his seventy brothers en route to establishing a brutal dictatorship. Similarly, the Turkish sultan Mehmet II introduced the practice of confining all royal siblings in cages until an heir was produced, at which time all the brothers were strangled with a special silk cord. My brother becomes my murderer.

Anna Quindlen gives poignant expression to her hate-obsessed relationship with her brother:

> The most vivid emotion of my childhood, the one I can evoke even now, is my hatred of my brother Bob. Truth is, the word "hatred," simple and powerful as a punch to the gut, does not even begin to cover what I remember feeling. . . . A virtual rainbow of negative emotions—contempt, loathing, disdain— that is how I remember my life with my brother. . . . There is something so pure and uncompromising in the feeling, like the taste of lemon or the prick of a thorn. It's almost pleasurable, actually, to think of it, in my today world, where I have learned to shave off the sharper edges of experience, to be ambivalent, equivocal, to compromise. I hated him. Oh, how I hated him. I can only tell this story because I now love my brother as fiercely as I once loathed him.[2]

Quindlen's accounts highlights how close love and hate really are.

At the positive pole is the profound solidarity, familiarity, and loving togetherness illustrated in the stories of Hansel and Gretel, Apollo and Artemis, Castor and Pollux, Isis and Osiris, and the twins Viola and Sebastian in Shakespeare's *Twelfth Night*. In the same savannah as the hyenas, lionesses—the hyenas' interminable rivals—enact true sisterhood. Prides of lions are organized around a band of sisters (and other female relatives). Males come and go, but the pride continues as a cooperative, lifelong sisterhood. Our lives as siblings, I suggest, are played out along this "cooperation-competition continuum." We probably learn more about loyalty and competition from our sisters and brothers than from anyone else. As one sister put it:

> I don't understand how people learn to live in the world if they haven't had siblings. . . . Everything I learned about negotiation, territoriality, coexistence, dislike, inbred differences and love despite knowledge I learned from these four: Bob, Mike, Kevin, Teresa. In some essential way, they were my universe, even more than my parents.[3]

Typology of Relationships among Siblings

There are few theoretical frameworks for discussing the quality of sibling relations. Gold, who studied siblings in old age, established five points along the cooperation-competition continuum concerning how close siblings feel to each other: *intimate* (deeply devoted "best friends"), *congenial* (warmly caring, but occasionally annoyed or competitive "good friends"), *loyal* ("blood is thicker than water" feeling, offering help when needed), *apathetic* ("never close even as children"), and *hostile* (keeping distance out of deep feelings of rage and resentment).[4] In their pioneering book, *The Sibling Bond*, Bank and Kahn developed a more detailed typology of "Patterns of Identification and Relationship between Siblings."[5] This framework is based on the degree of identification (close, partial, distant) and type of relationship. On the cooperation-competition continuum they distinguished eight basic patterns ranging from total fusion to unspeakable hostility:

- Fused Twinning: "We are just like each other. There is no difference."
- Blurred Merging: "I'm not sure who I am. Maybe I can be like you."
- Idealizing Hero Worship: "I admire you so much that I want to become like you."
- Mutually Dependent, Loyal Acceptance: "We're the same in many ways. We'll always need and care for each other in spite of our differences."
- Dynamic Independent, Constructive Dialectic: "We're alike but different. This is challenging and creates opportunities for both of us to grow."
- Hostile Dependent, Destructive Dialectic: "We're different in many ways. We don't particularly like one another, but we need each other anyway."
- Rigidly Differentiated, Polarized Rejection: "You're so different from me. I don't want to depend on you and I never want to become like you."
- Disowned, De-identifying: "We're totally different from one another. I don't need you, don't like you, and don't care if I never see you again."

A contemporary Israeli author, Benjamin Tammuz, describes an extreme case of a shadow brother illustrating fused twinning:

> I have always wanted whatever my brother wanted, and all my life I have envied him and tried to imitate him . . .
>
> Don't I exist at all? Can it be possible that I am only my brother's dream?[6]

Leo Tolstoy's early relationship with his brother Sergei exemplifies blurred merging. Tolstoy confessed: "I copied him. I loved him. I wanted to be him."[7] The great tragedy is that all too often brothers and sisters have very different emotional attitudes toward each other. One may be idealizing a sibling, while the other is de-identifying, wanting only to go his or her own way; another may be hostile dependent while dealing with a sibling who is trying to merge. Siblings are often involved in a complicated and wounding dance of intimacy. Only if siblings are both mutually dependent or dynamically independent can they achieve a happy equilibrium.

Sibling relations are far from static and may change in dramatic ways during the life cycle. As we shall see in chapter 3, Cain's relationship with his brother moves from mutual dependency and loyal acceptance to hostile dependency, then polarized rejection, and finally disowned de-identification.

> *Our families are like houses; you get the room that is not*
> *yet filled.*
> Kelsh and Quindlen, Siblings, 37.

Family Niches, Polarized Identity, and Dethronement

Sisters and brothers have more in common than any other human beings. They share a common genetic heritage and a home environment. They have both nature and nurture in common. Theory, therefore, would predict that siblings are very similar. Yet behavioral geneticists discovered that, by almost all measures, brothers and sisters are no more similar than strangers. These findings are a major challenge to the reigning paradigm. It is urgent that we understand the question "Why are children in the same family so different from one another?"[8]

One of the most convincing answers to this question derives from Frank Sulloway's influential, *Born to Rebel: Birth Order, Family Dynamics and Creative Lives*. To explain the striking differences between siblings, Sulloway uses an analogy not from psychology but from the ecology of niches in evolutionary biology.

Brothers and sisters simultaneously do and do not live in the same family. A firstborn entering the family has the ability to choose any niche, and most opt for a niche typical of firstborns. A second-born enters a family with at least one niche occupied and, if the firstborn niche is occupied, must look elsewhere. If, for reasons of temperament, disability, or illness, the eldest does not occupy the firstborn niche, that niche becomes available to a laterborn, who may then develop the "bossy" traits characteristic of a typical firstborn. The relationship between siblings will be determined largely by the relative position of occupied niches within the family system. Each sibling also gets a set of parents whose age, experience, wealth, and happiness at the time of the birth differ from those at the birth of each other child. To paraphrase Heraclitus: "You can never enter the same family twice."

When the niches are mutually exclusive, each sibling will develop a "polarized identity" toward the others. If one is bad, the other will be good; if one is judged beautiful, the other will strive to hide the fact that she feels ugly, perhaps becoming studious. If one is mother's favorite, the other will be father's, and the next nobody's. Each sibling is formed in the shadow of another; the identity of one becomes the negative identity of the other. Such a polarized identity unconsciously takes the form "I am not what you are." The polarization will be most extreme for "high access siblings," those similar in age and gender, who have the greatest need to differentiate from each other.

The occupant of the firstborn niche tends to adopt parental values, to embody and carry out parental expectations and therefore to be high achievers. Sulloway explains why firstborns are more likely to exhibit anger and vengefulness:

Firstborns have more reason than laterborns to be jealous of their siblings. Every firstborn begins life with one hundred percent of parental investment. For laterborns, who share parental investment from the beginning, the reduction in parental care owing to a new sibling is never suffered to the same degree. Parents may try to discourage jealousy, and firstborns may often suppress this trait. Still, when parents are not watching, a firstborn's display of rage can be an effective way of intimidating younger siblings. . . . Siblings, to their parents' chagrin, are often obsessively concerned with distributive justice ("Who got more?") as a way of repeatedly assessing parental investment.[9]

Because they are identified with the established order, firstborns tend to be more conservative, more willing to assert their authority, and less open to new experiences. Younger children come into a family with other children and therefore tend to have better social and interpersonal skills. They are more open to experience, to travel, to new ideas and to revolutionary ideologies, which imply an overthrow of the established order. Youngest children have the luxury of not having to grow up when another baby is born but also the danger that they will never grow or never overcome their identity as "the baby" in the eyes of older siblings.

In contrast to Sulloway, Alfred Adler, the first depth psychologist to emphasise the lasting influences of sibling relations, argued that under certain conditions a youngest child with a strong drive to prove himself may turn out to be the most successful sibling.[10] Youngest overachievers, such as scripture's most successful "baby brother," King David, succeed only when the traditional, achievement-oriented first-born niche is not well occupied. The prelude to David's famous battle with Goliath (1 Sam. 17:12–58) provides a classic exchange of the dynamics between an oldest and a youngest brother. Eliav, the firstborn, seeing David arrive unexpectedly at the battlefield, says:

> Why have you come down here? . . . Whom have you left in charge of those few sheep out there in the wilderness? I know your insolence and your wicked heart; you have come to watch the battle.

David retorted:

> *What have I done? Must I not even speak?*
> (1 Sam. 17:28–29, JB)

The eldest brother is bossy and demeaning; the youngest is struggling for recognition and status. Within biblical sibling psychology, one central tension is between a fixed sibling hierarchy ("I am first, and don't you forget it!") and a flexible sibling equality ("We are all equal."). In general, firstborns benefit most from hierarchy; laterborns tend to push for sibling equality or even to overthrow the established (sibling) order. The worst brother violence arises from conflict between sibling hierarchy and sibling equality, conflict that, if not resolved, can become intractable. Sulloway's study of scientific innovators revealed that firstborns such as Newton and Liebnitz fought bitterly and endlessly over priority but that laterborns such as Darwin and Wallace almost always were happy to compromise.

Research suggests that frustrated eldest siblings tend to have violent fantasies toward siblings. But they might not be the only ones. Moses, a supremely successful baby brother, may be seen to enact the vengeful fantasies of a younger sibling when he initiates the tenth plague and all Egyptian firstborns die. Symbolically, this plague enacts the revenge of a youngest child, not only on his metaphorical older brother, but also on the principle of primogeniture, in which the eldest son is favored only because of his place in the birth order.

The idea of niches also helps explain the sibling psychology of the only child. Because a solo child carries parental expectations for both sexes, the child must be, symbolically, both "son" and "daughter." The solo child occupies multiple niches at the same time. As a result, such a child is more likely to display both masculine and feminine characteristics. Solo children may be lonely in that they have no one with whom to share the inner world of childhood or to learn to take turns and mediate aggression. But this is not necessarily true. From a Jungian perspective, in the absence of real brothers and sisters, the solo child might compensate and develop deep relations with inner brothers and sisters, imaginary companions whom the child meets in play, dreams, and active imagination. Solo children who have a strong relationship to these inner siblings may never feel really alone. Only children who do not have inner relationships experience the existential loneliness of a world without siblings and an excessive attachment to parents. Some of the most powerful dreams I have heard about involved a brother or a sister of an only child. Thomas Moore[11] reports a woman's dream. She is about to be married but that her brother tries to destroy her wedding because he is in love with her. In the outer world, however, she had no brother. Helen Brammer-Savlov, an English Jungian analyst now working in Toronto, speaks of how these "night-time brothers and sisters" have their place in our psychic family.[12] She also tries to learn whether brothers carry the same emotional significance for women as sisters do for men.

Niches also might help to explain the gender effects of older siblings on younger brothers and sisters. A boy with an older brother, or brothers, tends to be more "masculine" (or more gay[13]); a girl with an older sister or sisters tends to be more "feminine."[14] In a metaphorical way, siblings often divide up the psychological space they share within the family environment. As we shall see, this division can take different forms, some destructive, some benign. In Greek mythology, Zeus forcefully, but successfully, divides the world among his brothers, Poseidon and Hades, and himself. Each brother becomes absolute ruler of his own realm, the oceans, the underworld, and Olympus. However, as discussed above, when psychological space is divided in an either/or manner ("Everything you are, I am not."), a brother or a sister becomes a shadow sibling. These shadow sisters and brothers divide the world among themselves and forbid the other to enter their psychological territory. Siblings who follow this course become dependent upon each other for an ultimate sense of wholeness. The shadow sibling is envied and hated for having those qualities denied oneself. The result of such polarization is that certain attributes, personal qualities, and characteristics are declared "off limits" and "out of bounds" to other siblings. Because sibling identity is based upon polarization, entry into the other's realm is perceived as a symbolic invasion or psychic war. If I am the smart sister, I must never try to be the beautiful one. To do so is to intrude upon my sister's psychic territory. But if I never invade her territory, I will never encounter the beautiful side of myself. I will live life cut off from that side, just as my sister will never connect with her intelligence. To live within the framework of polarized identities is to live in a fragmented world.

CHAPTER 3

Brotherly Love
in Two Indian Epics

To have a brother is to have a history.
Ricardo J. Quinones, *The Changes of Cain*, 7.

In chapters 3 and 4 I will use some of the most powerful brother stories in Indian and Hebrew traditions to explore positive and negative aspects of the sibling archetype. I will begin by discussing the brother tales in two great Indian epics, *Mahabharata* and *Ramayana*. Then, in the next chapter, I will do a close psychological reading of *The Tragedy of the First Brothers*. In these Indian epics, brothers who should hate each other show instead unconditional brotherly love and loyalty. In the Bible, by contrast, brothers start out cooperating but learn to hate. Together, these three narratives give a sense of the emotional range of sibling experience: how wonderful, and how horrible, having a brother or a sister can be.

Mahabharata

The *Mahabharata* is one of the longest and greatest epics ever written, ten times the length of the *Odyssey*. It says of itself: what is not found here is not found anywhere. The author, Vyasa, fathers not only the epic but also several important characters in the poem. The setting is ancient India; the central plot revolves around the five Pandava brothers, who struggle with their deceiving cousins, the one hundred sons of their dead father's blind brother, for control of their joint kingdom.

Such rivalry is reminiscent of what occurs in the more familiar story of Jacob stealing the birthright from his brother Esau. The Pandava brothers are sons of two different mothers. Living in a blended family, they look out for one another, functioning always as a cohesive unit. More typical is the story of Joseph. He also lived with half-brothers but with intense rivalry.

Mahabharata contains many episodes that normally would set brother against brother. Two may suffice. Arjuna, third in birth but first in battle, wins a bride, Draupadi, through a traditional archery contest in a neighboring kingdom. Coming home, he calls to his mother from outside their abode, saying, "We have a gift for you, mother." Thinking the gift is an offering of alms, the mother replies, "Share it equally with your brothers."[1] Because a mother's words are sacred in India, the brothers are obliged to share Arjuna's wife equally. In this unexpected way, Draupadi becomes the wife of all five brothers, living with each in turn, in serial monogamy. The Pandava brothers live together in fraternal polyandry, an unusual marriage practice still found in parts of India and Tibet. Miraculously the god of love enters the heart of each brother, and all five come to love Draupadi. Normally competition for a woman's attention is enough to bring out murderous passions, even in previously loving brothers. They can easily become trapped in the scarcity psychology of sexual envy and deprivation, literally or metaphorically at each other's throat. In this epic, however, sharing one wife seems only to bring the brothers closer together.

The second episode is, if anything, more dramatic. The eldest Pandava brother, Yudishthera, is addicted to games of chance. His behavior certainly merits a psychiatric diagnosis of "pathological gambling."[2] In Hindu mythology, any excessive attachment inevitably bring tragic results. Predictably, Yudishthera's deceitful cousins seduce him into playing a fixed game of dice. In the presence of his brothers, Yudishthera proceeds to lose everything: the family jewels, the palaces, the kingdom, his brothers, even himself. Then, when he has lost all else, he loses their joint wife, Draupadi. What is remarkable is that while Yudishthera is losing everything, none of the brothers criticizes him. This absolute absence of blame is most unusual.

Where we would expect tension, recrimination, even violence, we find instead compassion, mutual aid, and unity. Together all the brothers with Draupadi are exiled to live for twelve years in the forest, followed by a final year in disguise.

This spirit of brotherliness is repaid years later during their wanderings. Overcome by thirst, the brothers come to a pond. As they try to drink, they hear a voice: "Stop! First answer my questions." But four, unable to overcome their thirst, drink and die. However, Yudishthera, the last to arrive at the pond, restrains his desire and, through new-found wisdom, answers the Sun God's questions. When he answers the first correctly, the Sun God grants him a wish. Yudishthera asks not that his true brothers be revived but, rather, one of his half-brothers. He explains that his mother has one son living, but their mother does not. For his generosity of spirit, he is given a further boon: the Sun God revives all his brothers. With epic justice, the brother who lost all now restores all. At the end of the epic he is invited to ascend to heaven, but when he cannot find his brothers there, he says: "This is not heaven. Heaven is where my brothers are." He goes down to hell to be with them. In the subsequent "happy ending," all the brothers are reunited in heaven. The Pandava brothers clearly illustrate the mythic ideal of brotherhood.

The Ramayana

The *Ramayana* is the story of Rama, his beautiful wife, Sita, and his devoted younger brother, Lakshmana. The narrative opens when Rama, an ideal son and brother, is about to be installed as crown prince. True brother that he is, Rama asks Lakshmana to rule with him. On the eve of the coronation, however, Rama's father, the king, is forced by a second wife, to whom he once said, "I will grant you two wishes," to disinherit Rama and crown her son, Bharata, Rama's half-brother. Bharata's response is extraordinary. Instead of gloating over his great fortune, he pursues Rama, who has gone into exile, and tries to persuade him to return. Rama refuses, saying a father's word is sacred. Finally, after much persuasion on Rama's part, Bharata agrees to reign, but only as Rama's regent. He places Rama's slippers on the throne. Instead of struggling for power, these half-brothers enjoy mutual deference and deep respect.

In a second episode, Rama, Sita, and Lakshmana are wandering in the forest. An evil demon from Sri Lanka, the ten-headed monster Ravanna, covets Sita and, in an effort to kidnap her, prepares an elaborate trick. Sita sees a golden deer and, possessed by its beauty, tells Rama she must have it. Despite Lakshama's warning, Rama follows the deer into the forest. Before going, however, he commands Lakshmana to watch over Sita at all costs. The deer is actually a demon in disguise working for Ravanna. While dying, it imitates Rama calling for help. Sita, hearing Rama's voice, urges Lakshmana to go to Rama's aid, saying: "He is crying for help. He needs you." Lakshmana, recalling Rama's command, does not move. Enraged, Sita provokes Lakshmana into action:

> "What is wrong Lakshmana? Don't you love your brother? . . .
> Do you desire me so much that you'd have him dead? That
> must be the reason, or surely you'd rush to help him?"[3]

Lakshmana argues that Rama is invincible, that he was commanded to protect Sita, that the voice is an illusion. But Sita, unaware that Lakshmana has spoken the truth, insists that he is enjoying his brother's misfortune, that he is Bharata's secret agent and is lusting after her. Eventually he feels forced to go, but as soon as he leaves, Ravanna kidnaps Sita.

When Rama discovers that Lakshmana has abandoned Sita, he rebukes his brother: "You let yourself be influenced by her anger, and you deserted her! You have disobeyed me. Your action is unjustifiable, unworthy of you." Even so, Lakshmana's lapse does not undo their brotherhood. They simply regroup and concentrate on rescuing Sita. At one point, when Rama discovers Lakshmana lying bleeding and senseless on the ground, apparently dead, he says to himself:

> "What use is Sita to me? What use is life itself, now that my
> brother Lakshmana is dead? I can always find another wife like
> Sita in this world if I search for one, but can never find a brave
> and faithful brother like Lakshmana."

His words echo those of Antigone, the bravest sister in Greek Tragedy: "If my husband died, could I not find another to replace him? If I lost my child, I might yet give birth again, but since my parents are dead, will I ever be able to find another brother to replace my dead one?"[4] Lakshmana recovers, and the rest of the epic recounts their successful effort to rescue Sita.

The sibling interactions between Yudishthera and his brothers, between the half-brothers Bharata and Rama, and between Rama and Lakshmana are instances of averted sibling conflict. In the two Indian epics *Mahabharata* and *Ramayana,* brothers who should fight each other do not. They are brothers who truly act "like brothers."

Do brothers or sisters like the Pandavas or Rama and Lakshmana really exist? I believe they do. Among the most telling examples are brothers and sisters who independently survived the inexpressible horrors of the entire Holocaust, from Ghetto to Auschwitz, from death march to liberation, only because they had each other. Such loyalty and devotion in the face of profound adversity is the highest expression of what brothers and sisters can be.

CHAPTER 4

The Darker Side of Brotherhood: A Close Reading of Genesis 4

*"There is simply no Castor and Pollux in the
Hebrew Bible."*
Frederick E. Greenspahn, *When Brothers
Dwell Together*, 4.

The Indian epics reveal archetypal brotherhood at its very best. The Bible tells how brotherhood can go so wrong. To explore the fate of the first brothers, I want to do a close reading of the Hebrew text of Genesis 4:1–17. The narrative style is sparse and evocative. It uses scenes and dialogue "to display as fully as possible human behavior under great emotional stress." The text actively invites the reader "to imagine things not told precisely . . . a full description behind the actual words."[1] Reading Genesis is necessarily an act of "active imagination."[2] Hebrew tradition, in the form of the Midrashim provides numerous imaginative amplifications of the biblical narrative, filling in details missing from or unanswered in the text.[3] I will draw on this rich source of traditional lore. Using Hebrew hermaneutic form, I first quote scripture and then offer a sibling-oriented analysis.

> *She became pregnant and bore Cain.*
> *She said:*
> *Kaniti/I-have-gotten*
> *a man, as has YHWH!*
> *She continued bearing—his brother.*
> (4:1–2)

In describing the birth of the first brothers, these opening two verses of Genesis 4 reveal much about the psychodynamics of birth order. Cain, the womb-opener, is special. He is called not "Adam's son" or even "Eve's son" but "Cain," a person unique in his own right. The text, I believe, accurately reflects a mother's experience of her first-born as uniquely special, numinous, and holy. Scripture views first-borns, human and animal, as sacred and belonging to God. Exodus 13:2 gives clear expression to this sentiment: "Hallow to me every firstborn." For a mother, the birth of her first child is always the *origi-nal birth*. Significantly, Eve, not her husband, is the name-provider and identity-giver. As Erich Neumann taught, it is Great Mother who gives us our inner sense of fate.

Being first provides an advantage. Eldest sons are most likely to be successful, conscientious, and reliable and to take on leadership roles, as astronauts and presidents.[4] Being so special does, however, exact a psychological price. At times firstborns may feel they are born to fulfill the needs of others, to be successful, to look after their younger siblings and always be a model for them. Nor are they allowed to com-plain about the burden that comes with being first. Beneath a compli-ant surface they may harbor anger and resentment, a store that only grows as they are expected to set an example for those who follow. Firstborns must live up to intense parental projections. Eve does not say, "I have gotten a child," but "I have gotten a man." Eve, it is said, "does not see the child, only the man he is to become."[5]

Significantly, Eve's second son is born as a brother to Cain. The fate of every later brother and sister is to have a prenatal identity as "brother for" or "sister to" the firstborn. In contrast with firstborns, who are automatically, incomparably special, laterborns are inevita-bly compared and therefore have a *contrastive identity*. Eldest children must act as role models; younger siblings must react to them. In con-trast to Cain, Abel is given his name without explanation, showing how laterborns are much less the focus of intense parental hopes and projections.

The untranslatable, repeated Hebrew particle *et* hints at this con-trastive identity. Abel's sibling identity precedes his own identity:

"Who am I?" asks the firstborn and is told, "You are our first!"

"Who am I?" asks the second-born and is told, "You are his brother."

"Who is this *other?*" asks the firstborn and is told, "He is your brother."

The identity of firstborns is *self-referential;* the identity of later-borns is *brother/sister-referential.*[6] As if to drive the point home, the word "brother" is repeated seven times in just eleven verses.[7] In the identity politics of becoming a sibling, a firstborn must make room for a sibling, and a later-born cannot avoid being compared to the one who came before.

This brother/sister-referential identity is well illustrated by Elisa Albert, editor of the moving collection *Freud's Blind Spot: 23 Original Essays on Cherished, Estranged, Lost, Hurtful, Hopeful, Complicated Siblings.* Albert writes: "My birth announcement read: 'David and Matthew have a sister!' And I still reflexively frame my existence that way."[8] An extreme version of brother-referential identity is given by the contemporary Israeli novelist, Benjamin Tammuz:

> I was suddenly struck by the thought that with my brother's death, I, too, would die; for I was nothing but a kind of shadow: a kind of dream that my brother had dreamed. And when the dreamer died the dream would be over.[9]

We cannot escape our identities as sisters and brothers.

She continued bearing—his brother, Abel.
(4:1)

No separate sexual act is reported preceding the birth of Abel. Taking the meaning of "continued" literally, the Midrash considers Cain and Abel twins conceived from a single sexual act and continues the twinning theme by adding that Cain had a twin brother and that Abel, with a brother and a sister, was a triplet. In its succinct language, the multiple births are poetically summed up: "Two lay down, and seven got up."[10] In conceiving the first children as multiples, the text highlights the tremendous psychological importance of the brothers for each other. Such "high-access siblings"[11] are not necessarily twins, but they are of the same gender and are close in age and therefore pass through developmental phases together. Typically they are continually compared to one another in the family, at school, indeed everywhere. The novelist Ron Hansen recounts the difficulty of not being able to escape his twin brother. He reports that their scoutmaster rigged the election Rob won to become patrol leader because the scoutmaster thought that losing would hurt Rob's feelings:

> Walking home with Rob that night I fumed for a few blocks
> and then shouted in fury, "It's always going to be this way!
> You're always going to hold me back!" Rob, I remember, looked
> stricken. Rob is always Abel in my memories. I am always
> Cain.[12]

All sibling effects are heightened for high-access siblings. In contrast, "low-access siblings," in blended families, of different genders, and/or with an age gap greater than seven or eight years, have a less-intense psychological experience of being siblings. There is less kinship libido and more psychic space for differentiation. Cain and Abel are very high access brothers whose relationship and sense of identity derive from comparing and being compared. Brothers such as Cain and Abel have no escape from the psychological presence of the "other."

> *Now Abel became a shepherd of flocks, and Cain became a*
> *worker of the soil.*
> (4:2)

Like most firstborns, Cain chooses his father's profession. The dynamic of family niches is that if Cain is a farmer, Abel will search for a different occupation. The younger brother invents a previously unknown way of life that avoids working the earth, which was cursed as part of the expulsion from the Garden. ("Damned be the soil on your account." [3:17]) A well-known Midrash reveals the dangers when siblings cannot successfully divide the world into stable sibling niches:

> Abel said to Cain: "Let us divide the world between us."

Cain consented to that, and they agreed that all the soil should belong to Cain and all the sheep to Abel. Thus Cain became a farmer and Abel a shepherd. . . . Then Cain grew jealous of his brother Abel and soon began to quarrel with him. He would no longer allow Abel's sheep to graze upon his fields and he said: "The earth is mine."

Abel on the other hand did not wish to give his brother any of his sheep's wool for clothing, and he said: "The sheep belong to me."

Then Cain became furious and shouted out to him: "Pasture your sheep in the air, if you can."

But Abel answered: "Ask the earth to give you wool for clothing."

And thus the quarrelsome talk flew back and forth from early morning til late at night, and the wrangling never came to an end.[13]

Like Cain and Abel, brothers or sisters who share a room often have difficulty dividing up their shared space, saying such things as, "Don't you dare cross into my side of the room!" In a metaphorical way, siblings often divide the psychological space they share within the family environment.

Question: How do you get your brother or sister to do what you want?

Answer A: I beat him up, hit him, boss him, spook him, belt him, exclude him.

Answer B: I get mad, shout and yell, cry, pout, sulk, ask other kids for help, threaten to tell Mom and Dad.[14]

Do I need to say who is the older and who is the younger?

Dethronement and Usurpation in the Psychology of Firstborns

Firstborns are always treated as special by their parents, and they typically accept their preferred position as their "right." In many cultures, their special status is institutionalized, and they receive greater prestige and privilege, especially in status, ritual, and inheritance. For example, under the Law of Moses, inheritance gave an extra portion for eldest males (Deut. 21:17). Despite the overt ideology of preference for firstborns, the birth-order situation in Genesis is significantly different from that in the rest of the Bible. In the Law of Moses, firstborn preference rules. In Genesis, however, it is always the younger son who is chosen and inherits the father's blessing. Preference for younger sons is the experience of all the major fathers in Genesis: Adam, Noah, Terah, Abraham, Isaac, Jacob, Judah, and Joseph. This unique sibling reality has led some to wonder whether Genesis was written in the voice of a younger brother.

When a younger sibling displaces an older one, this process is called "dethronement." Although Cain is the firstborn, Abel and his occupation are listed first in the text. Cassuto, the great Italian-Jewish biblical scholar, argued persuasively that genealogies in Genesis do not necessarily reflect the literal birth order, but rather the order of eminence.[15] Abel, the shepherd, has displaced his brother as alpha son and chosen child. Cain has been "dethroned." The impact of dethronement should not be underestimated. It can leave a child with deep sense of wounding and a lasting sense of injustice. A dethroned child may feel a permanent sense of rejection and thereafter always be on the lookout for who got more. All others are unconsciously deemed potential rivals, seeking the throne. The text does not give direct evidence of Cain's reaction to his dethronement, but I suspect it lays the psychological groundwork for the events that follow.

> Any parent who even thinks of having a "favorite child" is
> guilty of spiritual infanticide.[16]

It was, after the passing of days that Cain brought, from the fruit
of the soil, a gift for YHWH, and as for Abel, he too brought—
from the firstborn of his flock, from their fat-parts.
YHWH had regard for Abel and his gift,
for Cain and his gift he had no regard.
(4:3–4)

In this passage the order of the sons is again reversed. Cain is "re-throned," restored to his rightful place as Son Number One. He takes the lead in offering a thanksgiving sacrifice to the Lord, and from this we learn two surprising things: Cain was the first person to spontaneously show a religious impulse and enact a sense of thanksgiving. At the time of sacrifice, relations between the brothers appear to be cooperative and harmonious, with the elder acting as a role model for the younger, who is happy to follow in his big brother's religious footsteps. Cain makes his offering and waits. One can well imagine how he felt watching the acceptance of his younger brother's offering but not his own, how he felt when he asked, "Why did God not accept my offering?" Traditional responses justify this Ultimate Rejection. The most convincing compares the language used to describe each brother's sacrifice. Abel brought "from the *firstborn* of his flock, from their *fat* parts," but Cain brought only "from the fruit of the soil." Abel's choice offering, it is argued, indicates that he sought to offer God his very best. Cain, on the other hand, brought only second-rate produce. Cain's inferior sacrifice reflected his defiant, close-hearted nature.[17] A more ironic commentator suggests, "If Cain had selected a better vegetable . . . how differently the future might have unfolded."[18] According to this interpretation, God was right to refuse Cain's mean-spirited gift. As a result, Cain "got exactly what he deserved." Such a "just-world" perspective, with its simplistic moral bookkeeping, does not work well in the ethical ambiguity of these post-holocaust times.

Michael Fishbane, writing in his seminal *Text and Texture: Close Readings of Selected Biblical Texts*, argues that there is no good reason why God does not accept Cain's sacrifice. This interpretation reflects the plain sense of the text, in which no reason is actually given.[19] This absence, I believe, reveals something profound about the psychology of the eldest child. These firstborns must renounce certain things in their younger brother's favor without understanding why. Because competition and rivalry between siblings is normal, the question must be asked: When does "normal" sibling rivalry turn violent?

Research suggests that the most serious and aggressive rivalry occurs when siblings are treated differently and that the disparity in the treatment, not its severity, is most telling.[20] As Murray Stein has written, "When a sibling gains privileged access to the Self (usually via a parent's special love and attention) and becomes so identified with it—as the favorite child, the golden boy, the chosen one—in the mind of the rival, jealousy and the usual amount of normal sibling rivalry turn to envy."[21] In ordinary families a child experiences a parent's rejection as divine rejection—as did Cain. One can imagine Cain's sense of divine abandonment. And he has a long line of successors in scripture, the last being Jesus, whose cry from the cross was, "Father, Father, why have you abandoned me?" (Matt. 27:46; Mark 15:34 citing Ps. 22:1). "Cain is an archetypal figure representing the experience of rejection and alienation."[22] Rejection can also be experienced as an act of aggression. A national survey in the USA revealed that 75 percent of children who severely attacked their siblings were themselves frequently beaten by their parents but that only 15 percent of those not beaten attacked a sibling frequently.[23] Parental violence is the royal road to sibling violence.

As those who usually benefit from the established order, firstborns often have "an especially high evaluation of power . . . Power is something which is quite self-understood for the oldest child, something which has weight and must be honored."[24] Firstborns understand power and often use it to buttress their special status, but when that status is denied them, they may feel desperately alone. Such feelings of rejection may well evoke "the schizoid position"—a terrifying feeling of being emotionally alone in an arbitrary, uncaring universe. It is the feeling experienced by a child in a world without a caring presence and hence without the possibility of meaningful intimacy. If Cain resembled other schizoids, he might well have felt that his love was destructive, leading him to hate and be hated.[25] Such sentiments are reflected in another Midrash, which describe the "words" which led to the murder:

> Meeting Abel in a field soon afterwards, he told him, "This world was not created in mercy; neither is it ruled by compassion. Why else has your offering been accepted and mine rejected?" Abel answered simply, "Mine was accepted because I love God; yours was rejected because you hate him." Cain then struck and killed Abel.[26]

If Abel's accusation is correct, Cain was consumed by hatred. As Philip Roth noted, "the danger with hatred is, once you start . . . you can't stop."[27]

In some respects, Cain also resembles the so-called conflicted-irritable child. "These children were fearful, apprehensive, easily annoyed, moody and unhappy, but more strikingly alternating between aggressive and sulky withdrawal behavior."[28] This pattern is significantly associated with authoritarian parents who rigidly enforce rules without explanation, while punishing violations harshly. They quickly show anger but rarely display warmth. This parental pattern closely resembles how God rejected Cain's offering without explanation.

I want to ask the reader a question: Did you grow up in a family in which there was a favorite child? In your current family, do you have a favorite child? I wonder if you know the correct answer. If you are able, consult your parents or your children. A recent survey suggests that parents are often unaware of their own favoritism. Most denied having a favorite child, but 84 percent of children surveyed felt that one or both parents showed a distinct preference.[29] On the other hand, when parents said they had a special closeness to one child, most adult children got it wrong when asked to name the favorite.[30] This discrepancy between the perceptions of parents and siblings is worthy of further investigation.

God as Psychotherapist

> YHWH said to Cain:
> Why are you so upset? Why has your face fallen?
> Is it not thus:
> If you intend good, bear-it-aloft,
> but if you do not intend good,
> at the entrance is sin, a crouching-demon,
> toward you his lust—
> but you can rule over him.
> (4:6–7)

When God sees Cain's fallen face, He speaks to him. His speech may be the first recorded attempt at psychotherapy. In the Hebrew, however, this text is one of the most difficult in the entire Bible. Even the Talmudists, those hermeneutic virtuosos, felt it was indecipherable.[31] Neverthless, the general sense is clear. God seems to be trying to do insight-oriented supportive psychotherapy. He seems to be saying: "Don't be so hurt and distressed. Here is your problem, and here are the dangers. If you have a proper attitude, you can overcome it." How does Cain respond? He does not.

Cain's silence seems impenetrable and defiant. Just as God did not respond to Cain's offering, so too, Cain will not respond to God's. In the language of attachment theory, Cain's silence may represent an avoidance of Him as a potential attachment figure. Compare Joseph Heller's inspired account of King David's response to the death of his child in his novel *God Knows:*

> In solitude, I was raging at the Lord, seething with scornful
> belligerence toward the Lord, and spoiling for a fight with
> Him. I really could not keep my temper. I wanted to have it out
> with Him, I was ready to curse God and die. But He would not
> take me on. . . . I received instead the answer I least expected.
> Silence.
> It is the only answer I have gotten from Him since.[32]

> *John Donne argues that "no man is an island," and yet*
> *that's exactly what Cain turned out to be: alone and*
> *cut off. Unkept.*
> Michael Dorris

A Therapeutic Response

God's first attempt at psychotherapy fails, as initial, clumsy attempts often do. This certainly was my experience. What makes the difference is careful supervision. Therefore, in the spirit of my own conscientious supervisors, I wonder: What could have been a therapeutic response for Cain?

I believe a hint comes from a subsequent biblical passage, which can be read as one of the direct responses to Genesis 4.[33] One such text is the golden rule, "Love thy neighbor as thyself." (Lev. 19:18, KJ). Most of us forget that this phrase is not an isolated motto but comes as a conclusion to a Cain-like situation described here in Fox's less familiar but more literal translation:

> You are not to hate your brother in your heart; rebuke, yes, rebuke your fellow, that you not bear sin because of him! You are not to take-vengeance, you are not to retain-anger against the sons of your kinspeople—but be-loving to your neighbor (as one) like yourself. (Lev. 19:17–18)

Leviticus warns against the dangers of silent, passive-aggressive withholding. Had Cain spoken openly of his feelings of dethronement, rejection, humiliation, perhaps, just perhaps, the brother violence might have been averted. Appropriately, a contemporary novel has Cain describe the brother-murder in terms of "the argument we never had."[34] The preamble to "Love thy neighbor as thyself" can be understood as an intertextual attempt to learn from Cain's example and prevent more murder.

Cain said to Abel his brother . . . (4:8)

In treatment, analysts pay close attention to subtle omissions that often point to significant unconscious material, like a fissure into the unconscious. The statement "Cain said to Abel his brother" (4:8) contains just such a lacuna. Cain's actual words are missing (as are King Solomon's in 2 Chronicles 1:2). Rashi, the great medieval commentator, tried to solve the omission by claiming that the phrase meant, "they had words." Many ancient versions or translations of Genesis (Septuagint Greek [LXX], Samaritan Torah, Aramaic Targum, Syriac, and Latin Vulgate) include the missing words,[35] "Come, let us go into the field." Why were these innocent sounding words suppressed? Imagine that the text had left them in. Anyone hearing such an invitation would ask: "Does this person mean me harm?

Can I trust this person in the field? Look what happened the last time!"

In an age when perpetrators use cover words to express unspeakable actions—"special handling" for genocide; "collateral damage," the killing of innocent civilians; "ethnic cleansing," mass murder—there remains an acute need to preserve the possibility of safe and honest talk. The suppression of Cain's invitation preserves the language of sisterhood and brotherhood. It lets us invite "brother" and "sister" for a walk in the field[36] without evoking an unconscious paranoid reaction.

The opposite of brotherhood is death.[37]

> *But then it was, when they were out in the field*
> *that Cain rose up against Abel his brother*
> *and he killed him.*
> (4:8)

The word for "field" occurs 333 times in scripture, but the specific image "rising up in the field" calls to mind the violent rape described in Deuteronomy 22:25–27:

> But if (it is) in the field the man find the spoken-for girl and
> the man strongly-seizes her and lay with her, then he is to die . . .
> *for in the open-field* he found her; when the spoken-girl cried
> out, there was no deliverer for her. (emphasis added).

Using the passage from Deuteronomy as a backdrop for Genesis 4, we can imagine that Abel did cry out in the field but that there was no "deliverer" to hear his cry. The image of "rising up" suggests Cain's desire to impose his will on his younger brother, to prove that he is "on top" after having felt "put down," to literally undo his dethronement. Our text, similar to Greek drama, deliberately hides how the violent deed was actually accomplished, unlike so much of contemporary cinema that glorifies the aesthetics of violence.

Traditionally Cain is portrayed as the prototype of the brutal killer. But remember: this is not only the first murder, but also the first human death in scripture. It remains unclear whether Cain really intended to kill his brother, or understood what death was. A contemporary novel written in Cain's voice suggests that the first killer did not know what death meant: "He [Abel] knew something about death. I didn't . . . We had no experience of it among ourselves. No one had lectured us on the subject . . . We had been left untutored in morality. I held Abel hushed and moveless in my arms to keep the life steady and irreducible within him."[38] From this perspective, the first homicide was not the prototype of many subsequent brutal killings but was unintentional, as when we say, "I'm going to kill you!" without really meaning it. Yet the narrative shows us decisively and morally that all killings are symbolically fratricides.

> Genesis . . . had to be the first book because it tells why there
> has to be God. . . . For if a brother could murder a brother,
> nobody is safe, all bets are off, and there is no future.[39]
> Arthur Miller

> *YHWH said to Cain:*
> *Where is Abel your brother?*
> (4:9)

God, as portrayed in Genesis, may have been an inexperienced psychotherapist, but He is an expert interrogator. Surely God knew where Abel was—just as in the Garden He knew where Adam was when He asked, "Where are you?" Why, then, is He asking? The question is not rhetorical. Rather it is to give Cain an opportunity to confess. Jung taught that concealed deeds act like a "psychic poison" and that confession is the first stage in the therapeutic process.[40] God's question offered Cain an opportunity to restore their broken dialogue. Cain's response is among the most infamous in all scripture: "I do not know. Am I my brother's keeper?" (4:9–10, KJ). The Hebrew word *shomer,* here translated as "keeper," has the sense of guardian or watcher. Note how God's question uses Abel's personal name and his social status, as if to establish Abel's full personal and fraternal identity. Cain's reply is impersonal. Without using Abel's name, he denies the importance of his brother to himself. Cain's question was designed to cover up God's question. "Am I my brother's keeper?" remains the dominant question for social life. What are our responsibilities to our brothers and sisters? Who counts as a brother and a sister? These questions must be stated and restated in each generation, addressed and re-addressed in each family, worked and reworked within the "family of nations." When we respond to Cain's question "like a brother/sister," we decisively renounce the schizoid position and, in its place, create a community of mutual responsibility. Our failure to do so makes us complicit in our brothers' and sisters' misfortune.

Cain's counter-question, "Am I my brother's keeper?" reminds us how Abel reacted to his brother's fallen face. Abel may well have acted like an "angel" sibling. Excessively favored children cling to parents as a way of protecting themselves from "devil" siblings who torment them.[41] Instead of fighting back, they appeal for help to their parents, who rush in to protect them, thereby reinforcing the angel/devil identities. Parental intervention often serves only to increase sibling aggression.[42] "These behaviors not only reinforced the children's view of themselves and each other as bad or good, they prevented the children from ever learning how to settle their own differences, as do siblings in typical families."[43] Such children become highly polarized shadow siblings.

It is possible that Abel did not know how to respond to his older brother's distress. Speaking in Abel's voice, the Israeli poet and Holocaust survivor, Dan Pagis expresses this inability to speak:

My parents invented grief
   I invented silence.[44]

Abel's silence gives Cain's words a hidden, accusatory quality. Cain's ironic question, "Am I my brother's keeper?" reflects his own feeling that Abel was *not* watching out for him when he was humiliated. Abel's silence weighs on Cain. It is the silence of all those who do not speak up in the face of a "brother's misfortune" but choose to remain silent.

I do not want to "blame the victim." Cain alone bears responsibility for his deed. But, as a "brother," Abel abandoned Cain when he was silent in the face of his older brother's shame and humiliation, when, in his own moment of glory, he failed to concern himself with the feelings of "my brother, the loser." Abel's silence then and Cain's silence later drew the brother-victim and the brother-killer together toward their shared fate in the field:

> *Now he said:*
> *What have you done!*
> *A sound—your brother's blood cries out to me from the soil!*
> *And now,*
> *damned be you from the soil,*
> *which opened up its mouth to receive your brother's blood from*
> *your hand.*
> *When you wish to work the soil*
> *it will not henceforth give its strength to you;*
> *wavering and wandering must you be on earth!*
> *(4:10–12)*

In the ancestral worldview of the Bible, a person does not exist primarily as an individual. Instead, each person forms the crucial link in an ongoing, ancestral chain. In such an ancestor-centered world, the worst of fates is to die childless. Abel's early demise means that he is "cut off" and will never become an ancestor. He will never "rest in peace" or, to use the traditional Hebrew phrase, "be bound up in the bundle of life." Abel's blood, crying from the ground, accuses Cain. Now God responds as the Divine Judge: What have you done! He calls Cain—and humankind in every generation (the Flood, Sodom, Egypt, and beyond)—to account for all bloodshed and every injustice. Cain must face his deeds and the cry of his brother's blood.

To understand Cain's response, we must look more closely at the Hebrew text of Genesis 4:13 and especially the Hebrew word *avonee*, which means both "my sin" and "my punishment for sin."[45] Many translations (JPS, JB, KJ) use "My punishment is too great to bear!"[46] This portrays Cain as a moral weakling, unable to face up to the punishment he so rightly deserves. He is an unregenerate, unredeemable murderer. Implicit in this view is the splitting of good and evil: Abel is the innocent victim; Cain, his remorseless killer. Michael Dorris describes this simplistic Sunday-school approach:

> In the watered-down morality tale of my grade school Bible Stories book, Abel was simply good and Cain was bad—that easy. The brothers got equal billing, were costars I was supposed to emulate. Later, as an altar boy, every time towards the end of the Mass that I recited *Agnus Dei,* Lamb of God, I thought sympathetically of that ill-fated shepherd, whose only crime was innocence.[47]

Such splitting of good and evil always makes Jungians nervous, because it is an attempt to deny our dual nature. Abel is the ideal sibling; Cain, his evil shadow. Instead of living in a dynamic tension with our own good and bad parts, we project our bad outward onto others—with disastrous consequences. Appropriately, Dorris begins his account, "I had the story all wrong," and goes on to note, "Viewed from a wider perspective, tales about siblings, often good and evil twins, abound in hundreds of cultural traditions—a way, perhaps, of accounting for humanity's persistent dual and dueling impulses."[48]

The alternative translation, which I much prefer, is: "Is my sin too great to be forgiven?" or "My guilt is too great to be borne!"[49] This version portrays Cain in a very different light. His cry is now one of deep and painful insight. Only now, following God's questioning and punishment, does he come to realize the enormity of his deed. In a Midrash that is quoted in the Qu'ran, Cain realizes the impact of his act when he sees a raven burying his brother:

> Then God sent a raven which scratched the ground
>   in order to show him how to hide the nakedness of his
>   brother.
> "Alas, the woe" said he, "that I could not be even like the
>   raven and hide the nakedness of my brother," and was filled
>   with remorse.

That is why We decreed for the children of Israel
That whosoever kills a human being . . .
   it shall be like killing all humanity;
And whosoever saves a life,
Saves the entire human race.[50]

This moment of realization is what Martin Buber called the "illumination of guilt," the necessary first stage in coming to terms with real guilt.[51] Cain's punishment, never being able to rest in peace, forces him to continue delving into his guilt. This second stage, which Buber called persevering in the knowledge of the guilt and which leads to sincere regret, is reflected in a Midrash: "He wandered the world everywhere rejected, 'til finally he slapped himself on the head and returned to the presence of his Lord."[52] For Buber, however, "returning" (Hebrew *tsuva*), as repentance is called in the Hebrew tradition, is not enough. He emphasized a third stage, in which the guilty party must enact a *tikkun,* or "repair" the guilt, at the place where the human order was injured. Can a killer ever achieve such a *tikkun*? Is not a dead brother "like water spilled on the ground that can never be gathered up again?" (2 Sam. 14:14, JB). A thief can restore his loot; a slanderer may make a tearful, public apology. What can a murderer do? Buber, surprisingly, suggested that even when the victim is dead, there are endless ways of seeking such a *tikkun.* The power of returning is conveyed in another Midrash: "After many, many years of wandering, Cain finally encounters his own father. Surprised, Adam addresses his son saying 'What! Are you still alive?' To which Cain answered, 'I returned and am reconciled.' Then Adam crying and beating his face cried out, 'So great is the power of repentance, and I did not know!'"[53] From this perspective, Cain is the archetypal repentant sinner, able to return to experience the full presence of the Self.

> *Here, you drive me away today from the face of the soil,*
> *and from your face must I conceal myself,*
> *I must be wavering and wandering on earth—*
> *now it will be that whoever comes upon me will kill me!*
> (4:14)

Many traditional commentators understand well the punishment of wandering as unending agricultural failure on an earth that is cursed. The medieval Hebrew Bible commentator Ramban understood this wandering in more psychological terms. He saw it as part of the process of returning. Having lost his peace of mind, Cain cannot stay in one place. Like the archetypal Texas drifter, he is forever on the move. What is clear is that his punishment makes him the world's first homeless person. Homelessness, however, is not simply the loss of a fixed address. It is the polar opposite of "home*full*ness."[54] A home provides a sense of absolute security in both its maternal and its paternal aspects. The tension between masculine and feminine attitudes is well illustrated in Robert Frost's well-known poem "The Death of a Hired Hand." Home is first seen in the masculine mode, by the farmer, as a place of logos and duty: "Home is the place where, when you have to go there, they have to take you in." Few readers recall the wife's more profound and maternal reply: "I should have called it something you somehow haven't to deserve."

The loss of the place one does not have to deserve, the place where you will be taken in, is psychologically damaging and disorienting. Homelessness, as Cain indicates, is also characterized by extreme vulnerability: "Whoever comes upon me will kill me!" (4:14). Being without home means being unkept, unprotected, unblessed. The contemporary crisis of the "homeless" surely represents a breakdown of our collective role as our brothers' keepers.

Why does God sentence Cain to wavering, wandering homelessness? What is the connection between fratricide and homelessness? Siblings, I believe, symbolize home. Brothers and sisters provide much of that unique sense of homefullness. When we symbolically kill our brother, cutting him off emotionally, or when we cease speaking to our sister, we lose our sense of being at home and at ease in the world. Home is, in a psychological sense, destroyed. Once we "kill" our brother or sister, we are permanently "on the run," in a state of eternal, existential exile. We never regain the sense of being at home in the world. I recall one man in his late fifties whose well-known sister had been killed while he was still in his teens. After that time, despite marriage and fatherhood, he never again felt comfortable at home.

"With her," as he put it, "I could sit in my undershirt. I could let my hair down. I could be a fool, and none of it would matter. Ever since she died, I feel as if a part of me is missing. I am really alone."

Cain's exile to a ceaseless wandering parallels the expulsion from paradise, only this time it is the paradise of living together in harmony as sisters and brothers. I believe that the image of Abel's body lying unburied in the field is truly the Bible's primal scene. Each generation of readers who encounter this shocking story experiences the psychic trauma and collective guilt of the death of brotherhood. The image of a murdered brother continues to haunt human history "unto this very day." Each reader is forced to ask, "Am I my brother's (sister's) keeper?" Primal events have a timeless, mythic quality; they repeat themselves endlessly. The trauma does not reside in the past but, rather, in a continuous present. They feel as though they are still happening.

I felt as though part of my soul had been cut away.

To lose a brother is to lose someone with whom you can share the experience of growing old.

The Lost Brother

Abel's murder, reverberating throughout Genesis, initiates the archetypal theme of the "lost brother." Loss of a brother or sister is the key archetypal experience that touches all the heroes in Genesis. Almost every character literally or symbolically loses a brother or a sister. Again and again the reader is confronted with literal or symbolic "sibling loss"—the biblical equivalent of the Oedipal drama.[55] The death, or mere absence, of a brother or sister has a profound impact on the identity of the surviving siblings. The loss of a beloved, supportive, ideal sibling may have a particularly profound effect. Even when siblings were alienated, a surviving sister or brother may discover that "someone I did not know I loved had died, some one I did not want to love had died, and that dying had a closed-door quality to it, a falling-off-the-horizon quality to it, the end, an end, nothing."[56] Another sister writes in a similar vein: "Siblings may be ambivalent about their relationships in life, but in death the power of their bond strangles the surviving heart . . . Were you close? Yes, but we didn't know it then."[57] Only when her brother is gone does this bereaved sister realize what her crazy "kid brother" meant to her. I suspect that only when Abel was dead did Cain really understand the significance of his brother.

Unlike the Garden of Eden, with its speaking snakes and magical trees, the world of Cain and Abel is fundamentally like our own. Yet it has special status, as the setting for the first and defining event of human history. A paraphrase might be, "In the beginning were brothers, and then . . . there was brother-murder." Much of what follows in scripture, I will argue, can be viewed as a response to the consequences of this primal sin. If the Garden story deals with our psychological prehistory, then the story of the First Brothers is concerned with the "interhuman," to use Martin Buber's term.[58] In Genesis the paradigm of the interhuman is brother-to-brother, sister-to-sister. In the narrative theology of scripture, every murder is really fratricide.

> *To hate your brother is to be a murderer.*
> (1 John 3:15)

A Biblical Theory of Brother Violence

For some the story of the First Murder confirms the inevitability of brother violence. My reading is very different. Until the rejected sacrifice, the first brothers seem to be living together in peace. The fact that they offer their sacrifices at the same time suggests they are on very good terms. Cain is the upstanding older sibling, guiding his kid brother. Only when he is rejected and humiliated does he turn to "brother violence."[59] Looking at the narrative of the first brothers as the prototype, I believe, it is possible to elucidate a Biblical Theory of Brother Violence. Brother violence occurs when three conditions are met. First, the siblings have strongly polarized identities. Second, the siblings experience preferential treatment by a Parental figure identified with the Self. This heightens the sense of polarization. Third, one brother feels public humiliation and deprivation, and the other remains silent and passive (even if not gloating). At this point an emotional abandonment occurs. Together these three conditions may be said to constitute the Biblical Theory of Brother Violence.

When brother communities and sister societies undergo similar conditions, in which ethnic group identities are polarized (as for example when the "authorities" practice favoritism), and there is no acknowledgment of the injustice and humiliation, the result might be collective brother violence, such as an ethnic riot.[60] Clearly social and ethnic violence has many causes. My interpretation of Genesis 4 suggests that violent reactions, by individuals and by sibling-like ethnic groups, are rooted in a sibling psychology. As one author put it, "Cain and Abel have not finished killing each other."[61]

CHAPTER 5

Sisters Keepers, Brothers Weepers

Why have you ruined my life?
Anonymous

In this chapter I want to examine the sequence of brother and sister stories in Genesis as a psychological response to the tragedy of Cain and Abel. I will try to show how each of these narrative texts presents a distinct sibling strategy for avoiding the original sin of literal, or symbolic, fratricide.

Sibling De-identification: Siblings in Business for Themselves

The Bible is full of genealogies. Most readers happily skip over these lists of who begat whom. Yet much can be learned from studying their patterns and variations. Most genealogies in the Bible are patrilineal, including only the name of the father and his eldest son, as in the genealogy of Cain's son: "To Enoch was born Irad, Irad begot Mehujael, Mehujael begot Methusael, Methusael begot Lamech." (4:18).

Then, six generations after Cain, this standard patriarchal pattern is suddenly and dramatically broken for the family of Lamech:

Adah bore Jabal,
He was the father of those who sit amidst tent and herd.
His brother's name was Jubal,
he was the father of all those who play the lyre and the pipe.
And Tzila bore as well—Tubal-Cain,

Suddenly detailed information is given about the entire family: two wives, three brothers, even a sister. Each of the four siblings has a distinctive area of interest and expertise: herding, music, metalworking, and being pleasant and/or a singer (*Naamah* in Hebrew may mean all three). From the perspective of sibling niches, each of Lamech's children has a distinct, nonpolarized identity. They don't unconsciously identify with each other, as with shadow siblings. In a literal and symbolic sense each is in business for him/herself. Their sibling niches and identities exist independent of each other. As a result they avoid the sibling "zero-sum" game, in which—as it was for Abel and Cain—my receiving is based upon your losing. This strategy of avoiding conflict among brothers and sisters is called, rather clumsily, "sibling de-identification"[1] because no sister's or brother's identity is based on identifying with siblings. However, even as it protects against destructive envy and rage, the strategy also reduces the emotional closeness that Jung called "kinship libido, a kind of instinct, like a sheep dog which keeps the family group intact . . . a satisfying feeling of belonging together."[2]

An illustration of such emotional distance is found in a description of Charles Darwin's family: "The Darwin family *are* a nice family together, extremely nice, always cordial and kind together and yet it strikes me that they are like affectionate second cousins more than brothers and sisters. . . . Each goes his own way, thinks his own thoughts to himself."[3] The great benefit of this sibling strategy is the absence of intense negative feelings and rivalry between brothers and sisters. The cost is that little emotional closeness remains. Siblings often live side by side as "sibling strangers." This conflict-avoidance strategy leaves family members without an authentic sense of brotherhood or sisterhood. Families based on the principle of sibling de-identification know neither the anguish nor the joy that a life with brothers and sisters can bring.

*Those who are born in the wake of death, harbour a
silent scream in their dreams. Buried deep under the
ashes of another, they cry for a life of their own.*
Kristina Schellinski, "Who am I?," 189.

*These . . . are the dead, not just your dead, . . . but also
the thronging dead of human history, the ghostly
procession of the past, . . . I see behind you, behind
the mirror of your eyes, the crush of dangerous
shadows, the dead, who look greedily through empty
sockets of your eyes, who moan and hope to gather
up through you all the loose ends of the ages, which
sigh in them.*
Carl Gustav Jung, *The Red Book*, 296.

The Syndrome of the Replacement Child

The next example of sibling psychology in the Bible concerns the syndrome of the "replacement child." A replacement child is a living child who comes to take the place of a dead one. It is a strategy, once favored by doctors, to prevent the painful work of mourning by bereaved parents. Typically the replacement child is born soon after the death of another child but before that child has been adequately mourned. The replacement child comes to fill the void left by a dead brother or sister. The dynamic of the mourning mother is well illustrated in an excerpt from Victor Hugo's poem "The One Who Returned":

*Oh, mothers, the cradle is linked to the grave. . . .
Death entered like a thief and took him. . . .
The physician advised the father, "She needs a distraction
for her unhappy heart. The dead child needs a
brother." . . .
Time passed. . . . She felt the stirrings of motherhood
for the second time . . .
when suddenly, one day she turned pale.*

"No, no I do not want this! You would be jealous!
O my gentle slumbering child, who are frozen in the ground,
you would say: 'They are forgetting me; another has
taken my place.' No, no!"[4]

Contemporary clinical research has revealed that introducing a replacement can be harmful for parents and especially for the child. Replacement children often suffer from a confused sense of identity. They might feel, "I am someone else." Because they come into life to fill somebody else's shoes, they often do not know what belongs to them and what to their dead sibling. A contemporary case gives a sense of this characteristic doubt:

> Janet Farr was conceived just two months after the death of an infant sister. She was given her sister's name, Janet. Janet was never sure who she was. She would ask herself, "Am I myself, or am I the girl who died? Who is Janet Farr?[5]

SCRIPTURE DESCRIBES THE BIRTH AND NAMING
OF THE FIRST REPLACEMENT CHILD

Eve bears another son, whom she calls Seth, meaning "God has granted me another seed in place of Abel." (4:25) For Eve, Seth is a replacement child. Which aspects of the replacement syndrome Seth experienced we don't know, but it was a central part of his identity.[6] He may have asked himself, as Janet Farr did, "Am I loved for myself or in place of my dead brother?"

The parents' unresolved grief is folded into the psyche of a replacement child, who, as a consequence, may suffer a sense of emptiness and confusion. The result is that replacement children do not have an inner emotional space of their own. Their psyche is centered on an absence: the sibling they never knew. Even when they fulfill parental expectations, they experience a vague underlying sense of guilt, often a gnawing, unspeakable feeling akin to survivor guilt: "Another died so I may live," or "Why did it happen to them and not to me?" even "I live because the other has died," or "I am responsible for the death of the other. I have murdered the other." They may lack a sense of basic security as a result of internalizing parental anxiety ("lest this child die too"). In their own psyche they ask, "Could it still happen to me?"[7] Often when the child disappoints the parents, the absent child is idealized ("If only s/he had lived"). In such circumstances the replacement child may develop an unconscious murderous rage against the sibling it never knew. But the absence of a person on whom to focus the rage can cause much confusion for the replacement child. Many replacement children are unaware of their status because no one told them about the dead brother or sister they came to replace. In contrast, for some their replacement identity is paramount and explicit. Many second-generation Holocaust survivors, for example, are named, not for a single individual but often for an entire extended family. These "memorial candles" often sense that their life does not truly belong to them but must serve as an ongoing memorial to the dead. As a young man once expressed it: "My mother was in the Warsaw Ghetto, but she escaped. I was never there, but I cannot get out."

On the other hand, many famous and creative people suffered from the replacement syndrome. These include King Solomon, Ludwig van Beethoven, Vincent van Gogh, Salvador Dali, Rainer Maria Rilke, Sabina Spielrein, Harriet Beecher Stowe (author of *Uncle Tom's Cabin*), James Barrie (creator of *Peter Pan*), and even Jung himself—born after three previous newborn babies had died.[8] Being a replacement child might be a source of ambition and creativity. Such children might feel the need to prove themselves worthy and unique in their own right. As Kristina Schellinski argues, it may be the impetus for a journey toward individuation. This certainly seems true for Salvador Dali, who was born just nine months and ten days after the death of his brother, also called Salvador. He spoke of the burden and guilt he carried all his life. Yet this replacement condition was a great stimulus to his creativity and flair: "[In] all the eccentricities which I commit . . . I wish to prove to myself that I am not my dead brother, but the living one."[9] Writing in *The Red Book*, Jung echoes Dali: "The dead will besiege you terribly to live your unlived life."[10]

> *It is written in the Bible, "Honor thy father and thy mother."*

Sisters Keepers, Brothers Weepers   (53)

KILLING YOUR DEAD BROTHER

A variation on the replacement theme is played out in the infamous story of Onan, the middle son of Judah (38:8–10). In that strange narrative, Judah's eldest son, Er, married Tamar but "did ill in the eyes of YHWH, and YHWH caused him to die." (38:7) Because Er died childless, his younger brother, Onan, was called upon to "preserve seed for [his] brother!" by marrying Tamar. This practice, called the levirate, was designed to provide a replacement heir for a dead brother, as described in Deuteronomy: "When brothers dwell together and one of them dies, and a son he does not have, the wife of the dead-man is not to go outside [in marriage], to a strange man: her brother-in-law is to come to her and take her for himself as a wife, doing-the-brother-in-law's-duty by her. Now it shall be that the firstborn that she bears will be established under the name of his dead brother, that his name not be blotted-out from Israel." (25:5–6) But Onan, instead of fathering this replacement son who would be his older brother's son and heir, defies his dead brother by his infamous act of coitus interruptus: "But Onan knew that the seed would not be his, so it was, whenever he came in to his brother's wife, he let it go to ruin on the ground." (38:9) The deliberate spilling of his seed is nothing less than a double act of murder: killing his own unborn children and his brother's posterity. Without a surrogate heir or posthumous son, Er is "cut off," a fate the Bible considered worse than death itself. In killing his brother's unborn child, Onan acted like a replacement who can have an identity of his own only by "killing the dead."[11] Onan's actions show how a sibling's murderous feelings and refusal to become a replacement can continue even when one of them is dead.

THE DESTRUCTION OF BROTHERHOOD AND PERMANENT INEQUALITY

The next set of brothers is the three sons of Noah: Shem, Ham, and Japheth. Together these brothers survived the Flood, in which the rest of humanity was killed. Shared adversity often strengthens a feeling of brotherhood, a sense of solidarity, among survivors. But for this threesome the opposite occurs. One shocking incident brings about lasting inequality that destroys their brotherhood forever.

After the Flood, Noah, apparently suffering from posttraumatic stress disorder, "became drunk and exposed himself in the middle of his tent." (9:21) Entering the tent, his youngest son, Ham, saw his father's nakedness. Although most translations of this verse say only that Ham *saw* his father's exposed body, the Hebrew phrase "to see a father's nakedness" is generally understood to refer to forbidden sexual practices. (The Midrash suggests that sodomy or castration was involved.)[12] Nevertheless, gazing upon a parent's nakedness was an act specifically prohibited by Mosaic law: "The nakedness of your father, and the nakedness of your mother, you are not to expose!" (Lev. 18:7)

After seeing his father naked;, Ham tells his brothers. Their immediate reaction is to restore Noah's dignity, covering him in order not to gaze upon their naked father: "Their faces were turned backward, their father's nakedness they did not see." (9:23) I suggest that Ham's seeing "his father's nakedness" can be understood not in sexual terms but symbolically. Seeing a father naked means perceiving him without the persona and aura of Fatherhood. Ham saw Noah as a pathetic, posttraumatic old drunk. Worse, he made light of it with his brothers: "Our father, literally and metaphorically, has no clothes."

Ham's brothers, horrified by his new perception of their father, are quick to restore Noah's father-persona. For them Noah is still the Idealized Father. It is this difference in perception of Father (or Mother) that drives the siblings apart. Consider a family in which a daughter claims that their father sexually abused her as a child. Her siblings, outraged by such an accusation, emphatically deny that he would commit such an unfatherly act. They expel her emotionally from the family, and the breach is never mended. In family life, I believe, some of the least repairable rifts between siblings result from just such split perceptions of their common parent.

Noah, regaining consciousness and hearing what his "littlest son" had done to him, asserts his patriarchal authority for one last and lasting gesture. In the patriarchal world he cannot punish his own son directly; in doing so he would only hurt himself. Instead he wounds Ham by punishing Ham's son, inflilcting a wound that will endure in perpetuity: "Damned be Canaan, servant of servants may he be to his brothers!" (9:25) The impact of Noah's curse is to create a lasting sense of inequality based on a permanent, public, paternal preference. Such institutionalized inequality destroys the very possibility of genuine brotherhood.[13] The defeat of such institutionalized inequality makes possible the restoration of brotherhood and sisterhood.

One particularly painful example of "institutionalized inequality" in family life occurs when a parent divides the inheritance unequally among siblings, or even cuts one child out of the will completely. Such discrimination involves public humiliation that intensifies any latent rift between sisters and brothers and might break the sibling bond altogether. I recall two situations in which a wealthy father deliberately cut a daughter out of the family will. The disinherited daughter appeared before her sister to ask for what she felt was her share of the inheritance. The sister refused, saying that she felt duty-bound to follow their father's wishes, that not to do so would be to betray their father, who remained the sister's idealized authority. The two never spoke again.

In the other family something different happened. As soon as the inequality was revealed, one sister rose up and said that their father's will was not just, that they must include all the siblings. She proposed that all the heirs contribute their inheritances to a common fund from which all the siblings, including the disinherited sister, would receive equal shares. So it was done. In this way, sisterhood was saved.

> *To lose a brother is to lose someone with whom you can*
> *share the experience of growing old, who is supposed*
> *to bring you a sister-in-law and nieces and nephews,*
> *creatures to people the tree of your life and give it*
> *new branches.*
> Yann Martel, *The Life of Pi*, 124.

> *They did not know that I had suffered a great loss.*
> Jamaica Kinkaid, *My Brother*, 155–56.

I am my brother's death.
    Elizabeth DeTiva-Raeburn, writing about death of
        her only sibling at age fourteen.

THE ABSENCE OF THE SIBLING MOURNER

The next family group comprises Abram and his brothers, Haran and Nahor. Almost the first event we learn about in Abram's life is the death of Haran. The biblical text presents the experience exclusively from the perspective of the bereaved father: "Haran died in the living-presence of Terah his father." (11:28) Nothing shatters the ancestral order like the death of a child. Yet the death notice points to another phenomenon common in the psychology of siblings. When a child dies, the grief of parents overwhelms and obscures the siblings' mourning. Typically there is no emotional space for siblings to express the depth of their loss. Yet brothers such as Abraham and Nahor are no less mourners than their father. Because the siblings' grief is given no literary or emotional space, they feel that they have lost not only a brother or a sister but also a parent. The lack of public and social recognition of siblings' loss was felt acutely by sibling survivors of those killed in the World Trade Center on 9/11 who were excluded from all notification, police contact, legal involvement, and compensation.[14] They were "disenfranchised mourners."[15]

Until recently, even though the Judaic obligation to mourn for a brother or sister is the same as for a spouse, a parent, or a child, the State of Israel afforded no social or public recognition of the siblings' loss. Beginning in 1981, however, brothers and sisters of dead soldiers were recognized and given access to psychological services previously available only to parents. Much of my understanding of the enormous impact of the death of a brother and sister comes from working with these bereaved siblings. If brothers and sisters, as I argued, symbolize home and security, then the death of a sibling produces disorientation and fragmentation. The loss of a sibling creates a world that is lonely, fractured, and unredeemed.

Abraham's next "sibling-like" episode reveals his relationship with Lot, the son of this dead brother. Abraham had adopted Lot and become his "replacement father." From the perspective of Western kinship, Abraham and Lot are uncle and nephew, but in biblical Hebrew they are called *akhim,* which Fox translates here as "brother-men."

Eventually Abraham and Lot grow so wealthy that an eco-crisis results. The land can no longer support their huge flocks. Quarrels break out between their respective herdsmen. Despite their being brother-men, Abraham sees the need for preemptive action through a separation by agreement. To forestall resentments that might lead to a "hierarchy conflict," Abraham, an archetypally wise older brother, gives first choice to his junior partner: "Is not all the land before you? Pray part from me! If to the left, then I to the right, If to the right, then I to the left."[16] (13:8–9) Abraham institutes the principle of "taking turns," so important in the lives of siblings old and young. Taking turns is not always a simple matter. Disputes between young children about taking turns are more liable even than disputes between parent and child to end in tears and angry outbursts.[17] Abraham transforms a competitive "scarcity" psychology ("There's not enough to go around; I must grab what I can regardless of whether it's at your expense.") into a cooperative "surplus" psychology ("If we share wisely, there will be more than enough to go around."). A conscious separation involves a willing sacrifice, a theme Jung felt was vital to development of the personality. Such a "separation by agreement" strategy allows a strong sense of mutual responsibility among brothers and sisters, even if they live far apart.

Siblings may feel close to each other even if they rarely see each other. They can always be counted on in an emergency. Abraham is just such an "emergency brother" when he rescues Lot from captivity in a daring nighttime raid.[18] David Lynch's movie *Straight Story* revolves around such an emergency sibling, Alvin Straight. When Alvin learns that his brother, with whom he has not spoken for years, has had a serious stroke, he feels an urgent need to see him. With a profound and stubborn self-reliance (which undoubtedly had contributed to their rift), Alvin refuses to be driven or to go by public transport.

Instead he travels on his own, across Iowa and into Wisconsin, riding a lawn mower. At one point on this epic journey, he gives poignant expression to the feeling of an emergency sibling:

> I haven't seen my brother for ten years. . . . My brother and
> I said some unforgivable things last time we met. I'm trying
> to put that behind me. And this trip is a hard swallow on my
> pride. I just hope I'm not too late. A brother's a brother![19]

Separation by agreement is a sibling strategy that prevents conflict but allows siblings, when necessary, to be "sisters' and brothers' keepers." The separation is based on an unspoken agreement: "Even though we rarely see each other, we are still brothers and sisters, ready to do anything for each other in a real crisis." It is a relationship persisting outside the touch of time. Separation by agreement does provide a lasting, if strictly limited, sense of sisterhood and brotherhood. Significantly, after the dramatic rescue, Abraham never sees Lot again.

Forced Separation of Brothers

In sharp contrast to this voluntary separation, the next brother dynamic involves the forced separation of Abraham's sons Isaac and Ishmael. The sibling crisis occurs at the celebration feast for the newly weaned miracle child, Isaac, son of Abraham's official wife Sarah. Sarah sees Ishmael, "the son of Hagar the Egyptian-woman playing with her Isaac." (21:9, JB) In a parallel to the opening of *Ramayana*, Sarah demands that Abraham expel her surrogate son, Ishmael. Significantly, it is an act most likely prohibited by the subsequent Law of Moses (Deut. 21:15–17). Sarah's motivation is not revealed, but she does seem possessed by the evil-stepmother complex: hating her nonbiological son and forcing her husband to disinherit him in favor of her biological son. It is a pattern all too familiar in fairy tales and second marriages. What bothered Sarah most, I believe, was that the playful intimacy between the brothers (which the Midrash maliciously interprets as homoerotic) threatens her brutal plan. Abraham knew that expelling his firstborn son was wrong: "The matter was exceedingly bad in his eyes because of his son." (21:11) With divine encouragement, however, he sends Ishmael and his mother away with only a bit of bread and a skin of water.

The text does not directly address the impact of this forced separation on the two playful brothers, but I believe that Isaac, the younger brother, was deeply affected. Hints in the text support such an idea. For example, he first meets Rebecca, his bride-to-be, at "the Well of the Living-One Who-Sees-Me." (24:62) And then, after his father's death, "the Well of the Living-One Who-Sees-Me" becomes his place of permanent residence. (25:11) This well is the only place in scripture intimately associated with Ishmael. (16:14) What drew Isaac to this very place? I believe that the Well of the Living-One Who-Sees-Me served as a "sibling linking object"[20] and that his return expressed his unconscious yearning to reconnect with his lost brother, what might be called "sibling nostalgia" or an "eternal longing for a lost sibling."[21] I suggest that he felt most "at home" there because he could symbolically reconnect with the experience of having been, and being, a brother.

Ishmael may also have experienced a sibling bond. Upon naming him Ishmael ("God hears"), the angel of the Lord sets forth his destiny: "He shall be a wild-ass of a man, his hand against all, hand of all against him." (16:12) This is the wild, indiscriminate anger of a neglected child. But the angel continues: "Yet in the presence of all his brothers shall he dwell." (16:12) The presence of brothers can provide an emotional counterweight to unfocused aggression. Dwelling in the literal or symbolic presence of sisters or brothers can soothe the existential insecurity of being a rejected outsider.

> *I would never have guessed in a million years how my relationship to my sister would change after my mother's death.*
> Rosalie Siegel

How the Death of a Parent Affects the Sibling Bond

The death of a parent often has a profound effect on sibling survivors. It can bring them closer together or lead to bitter infighting and even unrepairable alienation. In Genesis are examples of each. The death of Sarah removed the source of the split between Ishmael and Isaac. Consequently, at their father's burial they can join, as "Ritual siblings," in one reuniting rite of passage. Ritual siblings meet almost exclusively at funerals, weddings, and other formal rites of passage. Ritual siblings often share a rich past but have little current interaction beyond serving as symbolic representatives of "family." Their kinship libido finds little expression outside of these ritual occasions. Abraham himself showed his sons the way toward reconciliation as ritual brothers. Late in life, when he receives news about his brother Nahor, whom he had left behind, Abraham sends his trustworthy servant to the "old country" to bring back a bride for his son, Isaac. The servant returns with his brother's granddaughter, Rebecca. The marriage is a symbolic reconciliation between these absent brothers.

Alternatively, the death of a parent may remove the last remnant of kinship libido, even destroying what is left of a sibling bond. After their parents' death, siblings can become permanent, even hostile, sibling strangers. Patricia, a thirty-two-year-old single woman, felt that when her parents died she lost not only her share of the inheritance but also her share in the family. In an interview, she said:

> My siblings turned on each other and I was made the biggest scapegoat. My two sisters ostracized me and withheld heirlooms, mementos, and even my own possessions that my father had been storing for me. The pain of simply not having things that belonged to my parents has been startlingly intense, all the more because these things were denied me by siblings behaving viciously. . . . They have not responded to my efforts to contact them in a year.[22]

Another contemporary example comes from the film *The Godfather II*. Michael Corleone, youngest son yet newest godfather, discovers that "Fredo," his jealous, effeminate, middle brother is behind an as-sassination attempt. In a poignant scene, Connie, their sister, begs Michael to forgive Fredo, saying, "He is so helpless without you." In an apparent act of reconciliation of ritual brothers, Michael embraces Fredo, his only surviving brother, at their mother's funeral. But in fact Michael had been waiting only until their mother died. Now he ex-acts brotherly revenge, sending Fredo out to be killed in the very boat Fredo used to fish with Michael's own young son. Once their mother is gone, the last link between the brothers is broken, leaving Michael free to settle accounts. As one acute observer remarked, "When we are no longer sons, will we still be able to be brothers?"[23] A very simi-lar fear seizes Joseph's brothers following the death of their father, to be discussed below.

> *There are two things in life for which we are never truly prepared: twins.*
> Nineteenth-century American humorist Josh Billings.

Twins and Twin Identities

Sometimes sibling rivalry is so intense that it has the sense of pre-determined fate. The story of Abraham's twin grandsons, Jacob and Esau, has this karmic quality. The brothers are predestined, even be-fore birth, to become brother-enemies. Recent research showed that sibling conflict in the womb is not uncommon, that one womb mate may destroy or absorb the other.[24] Even in the womb, Esau and Jacob cannot divide their world successfully. When Rebecca is almost de-stroyed by their suicidal intrauterine struggles, she cries, "If this is the way of it, why go on living?" (25:22, JB) In desperation she consults an oracle, who says, "The elder shall be servant to younger." (25:23) To Rebecca the triumph of the younger over the elder means the per-manent dethronement and reversal of sibling hierarchy. And the de-thronement pattern is repeated—in the birth of Tamar's twins (38:27–30) and again in Jacob's tricksterlike blessing of Joseph's younger son instead of the elder. (48:1–20)

*"Mothers" and "fathers" were originally "sisters" and
   "brothers."*
   Lara Newton, *Brothers and Sisters*, 43.

Intergenerational Conflict

Parents often unconsciously recreate between their children the relationship they had with their own brothers and sisters. Isaac, for example, was chosen over Ishmael and had an ambivalent relationship with his "wild" brother. This experience might have led him to create a similar pair of favored and rejected sons, idealizing Esau the hunter and rejecting Jacob the tent dweller.

Rebecca, too, may have had unresolved sibling issues. When she is suddenly engaged to her faraway parallel cousin Isaac, Abraham's servant is eager to return without delay. Her brother and mother ask her to tarry for "a few days, perhaps ten." (24:55) Given the choice, however, she leaves at once. Her decision suggests that she was all too happy to get away from her brother-guardian.[25] Given how her brother later mistreats Rebecca's son, one may well understand her haste. Symbolically, then, the womb conflict between the twins is intensified by sibling dynamics passed down from the previous generation.[26] Parents who cut off their siblings may force their children to take sides in these family quarrels. I recall one young man saying, "I have never met my father's sisters. Something happened, but I was never really told what. It was too painful for them to discuss. I would like to meet them but feel it would be a betrayal of my father if I did."[27] The sibling sins of fathers and mothers are borne by sons and daughters, who must suffer in silence.

The twins Jacob and Esau are high-access brothers, each with a strongly polarized identity. Esau is a man who knows how to hunt in the field, while Jacob is a quiet, tent-dwelling man.[28] In one sense Esau and Jacob have successfully divided the world, but in another they are shadow brothers, deeply envious of each other's appearance, temperament, profession, territory, and parental love.

Genesis records two occasions on which Jacob cheated and humiliated Esau. The first was Jacob's purchase of the "firstborn-right blessing." Jacob is hardly acting as his brother's keeper when he persuades his "dying," hypoglycemic brother to exchange the firstborn blessing in exchange for some red stew. The second, more critical, occasion occurs when Jacob steals the blessing meant for Esau. When Esau is away hunting for food for Isaac, his blind father, Jacob, at his mother's insistence, dresses up as Esau. She covers his arms with skins to make them feel hairy. As a result, when Jacob approaches his father with a tasty dish that Rebecca prepared, his father says, "The voice is the voice of Jacob, but the hands are the hands of Esau." (27:22, JPS) Despite this paradox, Isaac bestows the birthright on Jacob.

Siblings favored by one parent secretly yearn for love and approval from the other, rejecting parent. To get this approval a sister or a brother might feel s/he must, literally or symbolically, take on the persona of the favored sibling. This yearning might entail stealing clothes, adopting mannerisms, or sneaking into the other's physical and/or psychic space. Such behavior is a manifestation of a "stolen persona." Children affected by this dynamic feel that the rejecting parent will never love and accept them for themselves, only if they are like the favored sibling. The stolen persona is poignantly illustrated in Robert Redford's touching film *Ordinary People*. Because the younger son feels he will receive his mother's love only if he succeeds as his older, golden brother does, he joins his brother on the swim team. Then the older brother dies in a sailing accident. The younger brother, who survives the accident, is convinced that his mother would have preferred that his older brother had survived instead of him. Not surprisingly he attempts suicide, acting out not only his own survivor guilt but also his mother's preference. Later, when he quits the swim team, he begins his own journey toward individuation.

Jacob seems to feel "I will receive my father's love and blessing only if I become (like) my brother. As myself, I will never receive it." Such polarized identity dynamics are well illustrated in a recent Argentinian movie *Everybody Has a Plan,* which tells the story of twin brothers. One, a beekeeper living in a remote delta where the twins grew up, is involved in shady, possibly criminal, dealings. He is dying of lung cancer. The other, a successful, high-powered pediatrician in Buenos Aires, is in the midst of marital discord. The brothers have not spoken for years. In fact, few of the pediatrician's friends know he has a twin brother. Then the dying brother visits his estranged brother, intruding on his neat life. Impulsively the pediatrician murders his brother, but then he flees to their home village and assumes his brother's shadowy identity. The confrontation with the shadow of his now-dead brother starts him on a journey toward himself.

Jacob's disguise suggests the depth of his unconscious identification with his brother. He literally and symbolically becomes like him, invading Esau to the very core of his being. When Esau returns to find that the blessing has been given to his brother, he cries aloud and bitterly, "Have you only a single blessing, father? Bless me, me also father! And Esau lifted up his voice and wept." (27:38) Esau becomes the Bible's first brother weeper.

His plea reflects a family atmosphere of emotional scarcity in which there is love and a blessing for only one child. What Jacob receives is at Esau's expense. In biblical context, the blessing of the First Born is a clear example of "scarcity psychology." Two brothers cannot both be father's favorite. I recall one patient who had a bitter memory from childhood. Her father was shaving, and she asked: "If Cathy is your best first daughter and Janey is your best youngest daughter, then who am I?" His hesitation left her with the wounded identity of the middle child—neither first nor last, profoundly nothing.

Displaced and deceived, Esau begs his father for a blessing. In response, Isaac gives him a sort of "anti-blessing" that seems to condemn him to a life of brother violence: "You will live by your sword, you will serve your brother." (27:40) Esau's fate is reminiscent of the institutionalized inequality among the sons of Noah. But the blessing concludes, "You will tear his yoke from your neck," (27:40) giving him the ability to fight back. The problem, however, is insoluble: hierarchy conflict embedded in a sibling power struggle. Isaac's words seem sadly prophetic of the interminable conflict between the "brother nations" of the Middle East, who are unable to divide the land between them.

In the biblical cycle of sibling psychology, Jacob and Esau reenact the polarized identity, paternal favoritism, and shameful deprivation that characterize the decline of the First Brothers' sibling rivalry into brother violence. They repeat the sibling dynamics of the First Brothers, but with a difference. First, the intensity of their conflict is modulated by the way the parents divide up their children. Parents often feel an affinity for one child over another, as Isaac did for Esau, and Rebecca for Jacob. Each such sibling is simultaneously a chosen and rejected child. Jacob, chosen by his mother, is rejected by his father; Esau has the opposite experience. The love that one sibling receives from one parent comes at the expense of love from the other. Each sibling secretly yearns for the "loving face" of the rejecting parent and secretly envies the sibling who has it. Such a "splitting the kids" family dynamic assures that sisters or brothers will become shadow siblings.

Second, Rebecca, seeing Esau's murderous rage, and fearful that she will lose both sons, sends Jacob to her brother "until your brother's fury has turned away." Seen against the template of Genesis 4, Jacob is a much less innocent version of Abel, and Esau is a much less impulsive version of Cain. Able to wait and plan the right time for revenge, "Esau said in his heart: Let the days of mourning for my father draw near and then I will kill Jacob my brother." (27:41) From a psychological point of view, the move from the desire to kill to actual killing is crucial. Esau certainly wants to kill his brother, but he waits. His ability to contain and defer his murderous feelings prevents a literal reenactment of brother violence. "I will kill you" becomes "I want to kill you" and, eventually, "I wanted to kill you."

Jacob, like Cain before him, is sent eastward into exile. The separation of the brothers allows for a cooling-off period, as in the ancient Egyptian story of the Two Brothers.[29] In the latter story the wife of the elder brother tries to seduce the younger brother. When she fails, she accuses him of trying to rape her (as in the story of Joseph and wife of Potiphar). When the older brother hears the accusation, he rushes impulsively to kill the younger brother. At the last minute a great body of water full of crocodiles magically appears between the brothers. The elder brother, having failed to kill the younger, strikes his own hand twice in frustration. From the other side of the water, the younger brother tells him to wait until dawn. In the morning, confronting his older brother, the younger says: "Why are you coming after me to kill me wrongfully, without even having listened to my words? You carried your spear on the testimony of a filthy whore!"

Then, telling what really happened and proclaiming his innocence, he leaves for self-imposed exile.

For Jacob, the cooling-off period, intended to be a few days, lasts twenty years. During this long interval, he flees to his mother's family, where he falls in love with his cross cousin (mother's brother's daughter) Rachel but is tricked into marrying her sister, Leah. To pay the doubled bride price, he works fourteen years as an indentured son-in-law. Then he works out a deal with his father-in-law by which he will be entitled to speckled and dappled livestock. When, as a result, he becomes rich, his brothers-in-law are resentful: "Jacob has taken away all that was our father's, and from what was our father's he has made all this weighty-wealth!" (31:1) The sisters, feeling that they have become strangers in their own family, leave without telling their brothers or their father.

When Brothers Kiss

After twenty years, Jacob returns to meet his brother Esau. Jacob, now middle-aged, was "exceedingly afraid and was distressed." (32:8) Fearful that Esau still has murder in his heart, he calls out, "Pray save me from the hand of my brother, from the hand of Esau!" (32:14) To appease Esau he sends ahead a series of generous gifts. Using the Hebrew word *panim* ("face") four times, the next verse shows how ready he is to meet his brother: "I will wipe (the anger from) his face with the gift that goes ahead of my face; afterward, when I see his face, perhaps he will lift up my face." (32:21) Left alone, as he was on the night he first fled from Esau, Jacob is ready to face up to all that Esau represents.[30] He wrestles all night with a "man." When Jacob sees he cannot prevail, he demands a blessing and receives a wound. More important, he receives a new identity. Thereafter he is Israel, the man who wrestled with God to replace the contrastive, polarized shadow-brother identity.

This "key moment" in Jacob's life story has many interpretations.[31] Symbolically he is struggling with his shadowy, unnamable inner brother figure. Previously he had struggled with his outer brother in the womb, during their birth, and for the blessing of their father, each time with a winner and a loser. In this wrestling match there is no winning or losing, no victim or victimizer; no superior or inferior. Neither figure can overwhelm the other. This stalemate is very much along the lines that Jung understood as "confronting the shadow." The man wounds Jacob in the thigh but gives him an identity to replace the trickster identity so polarized with his brother. It is as if he says to Jacob: "You will be blessed but only with a new name and identity!" The man, in effect, removes Esau's curse.[32] Having come to terms with his inner brother, he is ready to face his real brother, Esau, in a new way (a theme I will revisit in chapter 6). When the brothers do meet, Jacob gives his older brother the deference and honor he had denied him in the past, bowing down seven times.

When Esau sees his brother, he rushes out to meet him: "He embraced him, flung himself upon his neck, and kissed him. And they wept." (33:4) In the history of brotherhood, Esau's kiss must rank as one of the great acts of forgiveness. This is the first, but not the last, weeping-and-kissing reconciliation between brothers in Genesis.[33] Having met Jacob's family, Esau asks that Jacob join him, but Jacob chooses voluntary separation. Later, at the funeral of their father, the brothers reunite as ritual siblings with Jacob recognizing Esau in his rightful place.

> *We few, we happy few, we band of brothers;*
> *For he today that sheds his blood with me*
> *Shall be my brother.*
> Shakespeare, *Henry V*, 4, iii, 60–62.

> *Simeon and Levi,*
> *such brothers,*
> *wronging weapons are their ties of kinship! . . .*
> *For in their anger they kill men . . .*
> *Damned be their anger, that it is so fierce!*
> *Their fury, that it is so harsh!*
> *I will split them up in Jacob*
> *I will scatter them in Israel.*
> Jacob's death-bed "blessing" to Simeon and Levi
> (49:5–7).

Brotherhood of Arms: Simeon and Levi

The brothers Simeon and Levi reveal another side of brotherhood, the brotherhood of arms. Such a military brotherhood has both positive and negative aspects. The positive aspects include the enormous sense of togetherness and shared purpose that fighting men feel when acting in defense of shared values. In these cohesive brotherhoods, men are willing to die for each other, even more than for the "cause." Soldiers in such units feel a great sense of responsibility for their buddies. Research suggests that soldiers in cohesive units do serve as brothers' keepers: the more cohesive a military unit, the lower the rate of casualties.[34] For some men the male bonding provided by "brotherhood of fire" provides the deepest sense of identity, loyalty, and belonging they ever feel. In such units, men feel and act as brothers.

The negative pole of such brotherhoods is their potential amorality. Genuine leaders and international law place rational and compassionate limits on violence. Soldiers are required to function according to universally respected rules of warfare. Violence is regarded as an unfortunate, if sometimes necessary, means to a specific, defensible end.[35] When the "dark side" takes over a military brotherhood, violence becomes not an instrument of policy but a goal in and of itself. Violence itself binds the brotherhood together. They become power-mad perpetrators acting out a paranoid-schizoid group self. The cruelty, almost beyond belief, inflicted by military bands on civilians in Bosnia, Rwanda, and Afghanistan is such a phenomenon.

Jacob's sons Simeon and Levi exhibit an "evil brotherhood" in arms. In a strange twist, Shechem, son of Hamor, the prince of Shechem rapes, but then falls in love with and wants to marry, their only sister, Dina. Hamor proposes a marriage alliance via exchange of sisters. Sister exchange is a well-known type of marriage in which there are two unions, solidifying the bond between receivers and givers. Dina's brothers, however, demand that before any marriage all the males of Shechem must be circumcised. Surprisingly, Hamor agrees. On the third day, when the men of the town are still suffering the painful effects of circumcision, Simeon and Levi invade the city, massacre all the males "because they had defiled their sister," (34:27) and "rescue"

Dina. After they leave, the other brothers come upon the corpses and plunder the city. Jacob confronts the wild brothers, Simeon and Levi, in terms that seem to reflect more his fear of Esau-like retaliation than any moral concerns: "You have stirred up trouble for me. . . . I will be destroyed, I and my household." (34:30) Like most perpetrators, Simeon and Levi defend their atrocity, saying defiantly, "Should our sister be treated like a whore?"[36] (34:31, JPS) Their rhetorical question resonates with an Israeli cultural complex concerning a sister's honor. The Israeli version of the archetypally unfair question "When did you stop beating your wife?" is the following: "Someone says, 'Your sister is a whore.' Now go and tell them you don't have a sister." One can sense the emotional power of an imaginary sister!

In defense of their sister's honor, these brothers perpetrate a murderous attack, not merely on those guilty of their sister's rape, but on all the defenseless males of the town. Their actions go far beyond the demands of family honor, revealing a Cain-like genocidal impulse. Their wild, immoral action illustrates the dark side of male bonding. It is for this that Jacob curses them: "Damned be their anger, that is so fierce! . . . I will scatter them in Israel." (49:7)

Although Simeon and Levi function here as a "unit," they do experience one telling time of forced separation. During a famine, Jacob sends ten of his sons to Egypt to buy grain. There they unwittingly meet Joseph, the brother they sold into Egypt, who now controls grain sales. He accuses them of spying and will release them only when they produce their youngest brother, Benjamin. To ensure their return, he selects Simeon to be held as surety for the group. Why did Joseph select Simeon? One Midrash[37] suggests that separating Simeon from Levi reduced the likelihood of violence. Brothers in arms, whether in street gangs or in armies, spur each other to acts that neither would commit on his own. Breaking up such a partnership by means of forced separation might be the only effective means of containing violence.

> *The simplest relationships are those between brother and sister.*

Tolstoy, quoted by *Philip D.A. Treffers* "Foreward:
   Sibling Studies and Sibling Lore" in Boer and
   Dunn, *Children's Sibling Relationships: Develop-
   mental And Clinical Issues*, xi.

Brothers and sisters are as close as hands and feet.
Vietnamese provereb.

*My sister and brother were once my daily companions;
   now they have become a kind of granite, a steadying
   that nothing else provides.*
Nalini Jones, "Who Will Save Us Now?" in Albert,
   Freud's Blind Spot, 102.

Brother-Sister Bonds: Intimacy and Incest

In many societies the warmest and least-complicated relationships are
between brother and sister. Consider the following description from
Palestine:

Between brother and sister the relationship is warm and harmonious. It is certainly the relationship most idealized. . . .
Generally, the sister's attitude toward her brother is one of
love and respect, and his to her is one of lifelong concern and
protectiveness. . . . Love, tenderness, and mutual cooperation
prevail.[38]

Among the Swat Pukhhtun of Pakistan, the relationship between
brother and sister are affectionate and giving, while same sex sibling
relations are generally cool and distant, if not an overt rivalry.[39] Similar intense feelings of attachment are expressed by Russian writer,
Sergei Aksakoff: "My little sister I loved at first more than all my toys,
more than my mother; and this love took the form of a constant desire to see her."[40] The French author Stendhal, despite his many love
affairs, remained passionately attached to his sister, Pauline: "Every-

thing you say is in complete harmony with what I feel. You are my alter ego. . . . I love you with all my soul, I shall never love a mistress as I love you."[41] Lara Newton, a Jungian analyst in Denver, wrote that her relationship with her brother was "more significant to me than any other relationship." From the moment she came home from the hospital, they were a team, "companions in a mysterious adventure."[42] In many traditional cultures, the simple intimacy between sister and brother contrasts with the ambivalent feelings between siblings of the same sex, who have "relationships characterized by conflict, competition, and jealousy." I do not claim that all brothers and sisters do well together. I recall leading one dream group in which all the women spoke of abusive brothers with whom they had stopped speaking for their own protection.

The story of Dina revolves around the protecting brother-sister bond. The text tells nothing about any personal relationship between Dina and her brothers, but it reveals much about brothers as sisters' keepers. Simeon and Levi regard Dina not as an individual but as a sister-anima. In their imagination, whether or not Dina wished to marry the prince of Schechem is irrelevant. Her well-being is sacrificed on the altar of fraternal revenge and family honor.

> *Life is never dull with a sister.*
> Helen Exley, *Sisters!*, 29.

> *I feel closer to her [my sister] on some psychic level than
> to my friends or lovers; I yearn for a kind of exchange
> that is not possible without our becoming the same
> person. The extreme loneliness that results pains me
> more than I like to admit.*
> T. A. H. McNaron, *The Sister Bond*, 295.

> *. . . real-life sisters are a mixed bag. And . . . sibling
> fantasies are about as realistic as the colors rocks take
> on underwater. For every loyalty there is competition;
> for all the help you get with your parents there is*

> *frustration—on someone's part—of uneven or*
> *shirked responsibility. Everything real disappoints,*
> *of course.*
> Elisa Albert, *Freud's Blind Spot*, 241.

Sisters: The Best of Siblings, the Worst of Siblings

The Bible has much less to say about sisters than about brothers. Nevertheless, Genesis does contain two sister stories that are among the most moving of all sibling tales. These stories revolve around the essentially feminine topics of love and fertility. In the family realm, sisters appear to be the best of siblings and the worst of siblings. Sisters are more likely than brothers to feel close, share intimacies, and provide mutual support.[43] Sisters are also more likely than brothers to be in regular, friendly contact. Having a sister means never being alone. Lady Astor said that whenever her sister came into a room, it was like the sun streaming in.[44] On the other hand, sisters are more likely to experience intractable conflict and to be not on speaking terms. "Real-life sisters are a mixed bag."[45]

Love and Reproductive Envy

The story of Jacob's sister-wives, Leah's and Rachel, is the now-familiar story of polarized sibling identities: "Leah's eyes were delicate, but Rachel was fair of form and fair to look at." (29:16–17) The Hebrew word *rakh*, translated here as "delicate" or "weak," is an antonym of "hard." It may equally imply a visual impairment, such as "weak" or odd-looking eyes. Other translations are more psychological: "There was no sparkle in Leah's eyes." (JB) "And Leah had dull eyes." (SM) Whatever the semantics of Leah's eyes, the intent is to establish a contrast between the sisters' physical appearances and to have Rachel come out on top. Indeed, the contrast is immediately evident to Jacob. He falls in love with "the shapely and beautiful" Rachel for whom he works seven years. He goes to bed thinking he is with with Rachel, but when he wakes up, he learns that he is married to weak-eyed Leah.

The text gives no hint how either sister-bride felt on this strangest of wedding nights, nor how easily Jacob, the master trickster, was himself so easily fooled. A Midrash claims that Jacob was suspicious and gave Rachel secret signs to speak in bed. As a result, the "bed trick" was based on close cooperation between the sisters. While Leah was in the marriage bed, Rachel lay beneath it. When Jacob asked for the secret signs, Rachel responded beneath the bed. In an ironic twist on Jacob's deception, the voice was the voice of Rachel, but the body was the body of Leah.

The next morning, when Jacob found he had bedded Leah, he challenged his father-in-law to explain why he cheated him. Laban's response, reinforcing a rigid sibling hierarchy, was that in his tradition the younger cannot not marry before the elder. Such age-graded expectations still play a role even in some cultures in which such hierarchies are less formal. I recall a young woman who refrained from getting involved in a relationship that might lead to marriage lest that act turn her older sister into a spinster. Rachel and Leah's common husband binds sister to sister even more tightly, intensifying the polarized identities of older/younger, ugly/beautiful, and despised/beloved.

The tension between the sisters/wives heightens when the polarities touch on motherhood. The unloved Leah, who is fertile, quickly gives birth to three sons, whose names express her desire for Jacob's love. Her firstborn, for example, she names "*Re'uven*/See, a Son! for she said: Indeed, YHWH has seen my being afflicted, indeed, now my husband will love me!" (29:32) Only upon the birth of her fourth son does she give up hope: the name Judah makes no reference to her husband. Jacob's beloved Rachel, by contrast, remains childless. Because an inability to bear children is an unmitigated catastrophe for women in the biblical world, Rachel cries out to Jacob in "infertility despair:" "Come-now, (give) me children! If not, I will die!" (30:1) The Hebrew translated as "I will die" is literally "I am dead."

Because each sister's polarized identity and marital/fertility status creates exclusive sibling niches, each becomes the shadow sister of the other. Leah is deprived of her husband's love; Rachel is deprived of children. Each has a shameful sense of deprivation at the core of her feminine identity. As a shadow sister, each yearns for what the other has. The text says Rachel envied her sister (30:1); Leah, on the other hand, resented Rachel's being loved. Their multiple identities as sisters, wives, and mother/childless create a chronic sister conflict resembling the tension between the first brothers. Because Rachel experienced "acute reproductive envy," I suspect that she, like Cain, had unconscious murderous feelings toward her sibling. Sisters, however, are much less likely than brothers to express direct aggression. They tend to turn their anger inward and, as a result, are more prone to depressive, self-lacerating torment and depression.

Faced with infertility, Rachel adopts the strategy of surrogate motherhood to "be built-up-with-sons" via her handmaiden. This strategy triggers a new round of vicious reproductive envy, expressed in the act of naming. Rachel declares, "A struggle of God have I struggled with my sister; yes I have prevailed! So she called his name: Naftali/My Struggle." (30:8) Leah retaliates: her maid bears Jacob two sons. The sisters are involved in "psychic warfare." Emotionally they are at each other's throats and wombs, trapped in the familiar cycle of polarization, envy, and humiliating deprivation.

And now the text records a turning point. Leah's firstborn son, Reuben, brings home love apples, a fertility fruit that Rachel covets. When Rachel asks her sister for these love-apples, Leah uses the occasion (as recommended in Leviticus) to speak openly of her feelings of betrayal: "Is your taking away my husband such a small thing that you would now take away my son's love apples?"[46] (30:14–15) Symbolically acknowledging the emotional reality of her sister's pain and her need for a husband's love, Rachel proposes a bargain: "Very well, he may lie with you tonight in exchange for your son's love-apples." (30:15) This interchange is the beginning of a dialog between the sisters. Rachel "allows" Leah her conjugal rights; Leah "allows" her sister to use fertility magic—and (perhaps unconsciously) withdraws her "curse" of infertility. The result is positive for both sisters/wives. Leah has two more sons and a daughter (Dina), and Rachel, at last, bears her own son, Joseph. Instead of bitter rivals, the sisters become partners.

Lot's Daughters: Sisters Indeed!

The other sister story in Genesis reveals what can happen when sisters decide to work together. It reveals how deeply cooperation and sexual disguise can come together to create a truly exceptional sense of sisterhood. These two sisters are Lot's third and fourth daughters. Their story takes place in the shadow of the destruction of Sodom. Escaping with their father, these two youngest daughters reach a lonely cave in the hill country above the Dead Sea. Believing that their family members are the sole human survivors of a world holocaust, the elder sister proposes an outrageous plan. The sisters will make their father drunk, and then each will lie with him "so that we may keep seed alive by our father." (19:32) The plan works: each sister gives birth to a son, and these sons become the founding ancestors or tribal fathers of the Moabites and the Ammonites. (19:36–38) For the ancient Israelites, the folk etymology of the names revealed the incestuous origin of the sisters' progeny: "*Mo'av*/By Father and *Ben-Ammi*/Son of My Kinspeople."

This remarkable story highlights how intimately sisterly cooperation in Genesis is linked to the continuity of life. A traditional psychoanalytical perspective might see in this story the unconscious incestuous desire of daughters for their fathers, but that is not the point. The sisters consciously overcome the incest taboo, not for the pleasure principle but for the "life principle." Lot's daughters also display a refreshing, sibling equality. The elder sister conceives the plan but instructs and supervises the younger. Each takes her turn mating with their unconscious father. Clearly the elder sister is in charge, but the younger is an equal partner. These best of sisters are the only ones in scripture who engage in such genuine, active cooperation.

Sisters Compared

The contrast between the above two sets of sisters reveals much about the psychology of sisterhood. Sisterhood works best when tasks can be equally and openly shared, when the older is not more powerful than the younger but guides and shares her wisdom/experience like a big sister. Good relations between siblings are especially likely, as we shall see, when there is no "hierarchy conflict," when there is a mutual acceptance of who is "big sister" and who is "little sister," or when sisters work out an egalitarian relationship. In the Bible, genuine sisterhood is expressed through enacting sacred values of life, birth, and continuity together. Sisterhood is sabotaged when sisters constantly feel compared to one another.[47] The psychic constriction resulting from such comparisons leads to an unremitting cycle of shadow envy and shameful deprivation. Sisterhood is undermined when one sister has what the other wants but there is no way to share or take turns. Only when Leah and Rachel begin to empathize and negotiate do we see the beginnings of sisterhood. When the nameless daughters of Lot work together, they bring renewed life out of death and destruction. These survivor-sisters are to my mind, the greatest sibling heroes in Genesis.

> *This world is too wide and lonely to be endured without*
> *our brothers and sisters.*
> Modified from Pam Brown, in Exley, *Brothers!* 1996.
> 43.

Joseph against His Brothers

The story of Joseph and his brothers provides the most dramatic re-enactment of the archetypal story of brother violence, which we now understand not as an isolated novella but as part of a developmental sequence. As the orphaned son of Jacob's favored wife, Joseph enjoys a unique status. He is given an ornamented tunic or coat of many colors that in another context is clearly indicative of royal status.[48] Working as an apprentice to his half-brothers, Joseph brings "evil reports," or malicious gossip, about them to his father. The brothers cannot even be civil to him. Because he stays at home while they work hard as shepherds in the field, their sense of deprivation and injustice grows deep.

Joseph's dreams only make things worse: "Pray hear this dream that I have dreamt: Here, we were binding sheaf-bundles out in the field, and here, my sheaf arose, it was standing upright, and here, your sheaves were circling round and bowing down to my sheaf!" (37:6–7) And then: "The sun and the moon and eleven stars were bowing down to me!" (37:9) Joseph's dreams are transparent, requiring no interpretation.[49] Judging the dreams an expression of Joseph's narcissistic wish for power and adoration, the brothers said: "Would you be king, yes king, over us?" (37:8) Previously they had hated him for being their father's favorite; now they hated him for his dreams. Jung asked the fascinating question: "What is the opposite of love?" Instead of the expected answers, hate or indifference, Jung claimed that the true opposite is power: "When loves rules, there is no will to power; and where power predominates, there love is lacking. One is the shadow of the other."[50] Instead of brotherly love, their relationship is now based on a "power complex," on who is on high and who is below. Again a father's favoritism has led to a poisoned atmosphere between brothers. As Samuel Johnson wrote: "By exciting emulation and comparisons of superiority, you lay the foundation of lasting mischief; you make brothers and sisters hate each other."[51] From the perspective of Cain and Abel, the story of Joseph and his brothers has the feeling of a repetition compulsion. Like Cain, rejected brothers hate a favored brother. As George MacDonald said: "Love makes everything lovely. Hate concentrates itself on the one thing hated."[52]

I will not discuss Joseph's story in detail, but I will focus on a few incidents that transform his relations to his brothers in a way that recalls key breakthroughs in analysis. The first occurs during Joseph's first solo journey, when he is sent by his father to inquire into the well-being of his brothers at Shechem (the scene of Simeon and Levi's massacre). He arrives, but the brothers are not where they should be. There he is asked a question that is entirely concrete but profoundly existential, "What do you seek?" (37:15), and his reply sets his life agenda: "I seek my brothers." From this time his fundamental project is "brother seeking," striving to find his brothers in every sense of the phrase. It will take him many years to find them—and to let them find in him a true brother.

Meanwhile, when Joseph does find his brothers, in a field at Dothan, they decide to kill him. "Then," they add, with a bitter irony, "we shall see what becomes of his dreams." (37:20, JB) The brothers seize him, strip him of his fancy clothes, and put him in a dry waterhole. Throwing him into the waterhole seems not only a way of holding him but also a symbolic attempt to show him who is on top and who is at the bottom. Joseph looks up at his brothers, and they look down on him. Only much later, when the brothers themselves are held in custody in Egypt, do details of the incident emerge.

The older sons clearly intend to kill their younger brother. However, Judah prevents that ultimate and unredeemable action by evoking their shared kinship libido: "What gain is there if we kill our brother and cover up his blood? . . . He is our brother, our flesh!" (37:26–27) In fact, the word for brother is repeated four times in these two verses. The repetition has its effect, and the brothers follow Judah's advice. Instead of killing Joseph, they sell him to passing traders going to Egypt. Using the sibling dynamics model of Bank and Kahn, the emotional attitude of the brothers toward Joseph is Disowned, De-identifying: "We're totally different from one another. I don't need you, don't like you, and don't care if I never see you again." The brothers do rid themselves of the hated younger brother, but they do not regain their father's love. Instead, Jacob idealizes his absent loved son and develops a pattern of interminable mourning. For each brother the absent Joseph continues to function as a hated shadow sibling. In "death," Joseph becomes more powerful than he ever was alive.

Do You Have a . . . Brother? (44:19)

Years later, thanks to his skills as a dream interpreter, Joseph becomes an all-powerful Egyptian viceroy. In that persona he unexpectedly meets the ten brothers, who have come down to Egypt during a famine, desperate to buy food. Benjamin, the youngest brother, like Joseph in his youth, has been kept at home with Jacob.

Joseph the "Egyptian," in the magical position of "seeing but not being seen," recognizes his brothers but is not recognized, and he "spoke harshly with them." (42:7) As they bowed down to him, Joseph recalled his dreams of sheaves and stars bowing down to him. There are many ways to interpret this moment, but I believe Joseph felt a deep yearning for revenge on his hated rivals, who now will see indeed what has become of his dreams.

Joseph then concocts an elaborate plan to reunite with his only fully innocent brother, his full brother, Benjamin. As is typical of younger brothers, Benjamin is identified as "brother of." He plays a crucial part in events to come, but he is always the "brother of Joseph." As with Abel, Benjamin's voice is never heard. Joseph accuses his brothers of being spies, of not being who they claim to be. There is a symbolic resonance in this accusation, because they were certainly not being their brother's keepers when they sought to murder him. The brothers proclaim their good faith by telling their family story: "Your servants are twelve, we are brothers, sons of a single man in the land of Canaan: the youngest is with our father now, and one is no more." (42:13)· Their family history shows how much their missing brother remained a force both in the family mythology and in the brothers' own psyches. Joseph is still a brother, lost and sold but never forgotten. The story reveals how deeply traumatic sibling loss can be.

To prove their truthfulness the viceroy commands them, "Bring your youngest brother back to me, so that your words will be proven truthful, and you will not die." (42:20) He keeps Simeon as a surety until they return with Benjamin. With Simeon imprisoned much as Joseph himself had been, Joseph forces the brothers to experience anew the traumatic isolation and absence of a brother, to confront their guilt as brother's keepers: "Truly, we are guilty: concerning our brother! that we saw his heart's distress when he implored us, and we did not listen. Therefore this distress has come upon us!" (42:21) Only now does the reader learn the true horror of what happened in the field at Dothan. Joseph privately understands their speech and torment. He turns away, a brother secretly weeping. On their way home the brothers discover that their sacks contain not only food but also their money. "Their hearts gave way, and they trembled to one another, saying: What is this that God has done to us?" (42:28) Joseph's secret ploy forces the brothers to reflect further on their deeds. Aviva Zornberg, in her insightful book *The Beginning of Desire: Reflections on Genesis,* writes: "In effect, Joseph engages in a kind of psychoanalysis of his brothers: he asks questions that lead them to a knowledge beyond any they could have achieved alone. This is Joseph as inspired therapist, uncovering (the literal meaning of *gilah*—"he revealed") buried truths."[53]

The brothers return home from Egypt and tell their father all that occurred, especially that they must return with Benjamin. Jacob absolutely refuses, saying, "Joseph is no more, Simeon is no more, now you would take Benjamin." (42:36) Jacob's next response is even more surprising. He chastises his sons, saying, "Why did you serve me so ill as to tell the man that you had another brother?" (43:6, JPS) Jacob wants his sons to deny their brother. Such brother denial is undoubtedly embedded in his own complex relationship with his own brother, a person he cannot forget. Sibling denial is more common and more painful than one would like to believe, as illustrated in following passage:

> Do you have any siblings?" . . . Invariably, I open my mouth to answer and can't. After a moment too long I say, "Yes." Or I say, "No." The period during which I tended to say no was brutal, but it was easier than saying yes and then having to explain. . . . I could say, "I have one/two brothers," and then came a haze of heartbreak, and who needs that over dinner.[54]

Jacob goes on to highlight Benjamin's experience of brother loss: "My son is not to go down with you! For his brother is dead, and he alone is left." (42:36, 38). We have words for someone who lost his parents, or someone who lost a spouse. But we lack a term for someone who is bereft of a brother or a sister. Yet for some the absence of a brother or a sister might be a dominant fact of their psyche, as it was for Benjamin.

As the famine becomes more intense, Judah, having convinced his father that he is a competent brother-keeper, persuades him to let Benjamin go to Egypt. The brothers return. When they bow down once again to Joseph, he surprises them, first by inviting them to dine at his house and again when he seats them according to their birth order. The synchronicity of a stranger knowing their birth order forces the brothers to reflect on the meaning of such an uncanny event. It forces them deeper into the process of self-reflection. For Joseph, the seating arrangement is a recognition of primacy of birth order, a principle he had resisted in his youth. The arrangement also reflects another crucial aspect of sibling life: sisters and brothers know things about each other that nobody else knows. I am always struck by how siblings separated even by decades recognize each other because of secret memories. This is true of the amazing reunion of Holocaust siblings. It is true, too, of a sister and her brother who were sold separately as slaves in the generation following the destruction of the Jerusalem Temple and were reunited when their masters decided they should marry. In the wedding chamber they discover each other's identity via a mole on the brother's shoulder that the sister used to kiss when he came back from school. (Midrash on Lamentations 1:46) The powerful yearning to find a lost sibling is a theme that pervades biblical psychology.

When his brothers leave for home, Joseph, the cruel trickster, hides his divining cup in Benjamin's sack so that he will be "caught" and detained in Egypt when the rest of the brothers depart—presumably forever. Joseph's wicked plan succeeds! He is now in a position to rid himself of his "false" brothers and reunite with his one true brother. At this point, however, Judah asks Joseph, "Do you have a . . . brother?" (44:19) It is a desperate attempt to evoke sympathy from the man who, he does not know, is his brother. Judah's speech is complex. I will focus only on the brother dimension. Recounting family events since the "death" of Joseph, Judah evokes Benjamin's identity as brother doubly bereft, orphaned not only by his mother but also by his brother. Benjamin is Jacob's only link to the people he loved best, Rachel and Joseph. Then he offers himself as a replacement for Benjamin.

Something in Judah's speech touches Joseph and transforms him. I believe the key lies in the last line of Judah's speech: "How indeed could I go back to my father and not have the boy with me? I could not bear to see the misery that would overwhelm my father." (44:34, JB) Judah, is speaking of Benjamin but might easily have been speaking of Joseph, evoking the experience of having returned empty-handed and witnessed his father's reaction to the loss. Only now does

Joseph realize what happened when his brothers returned to their father without him, what anguish they met in their father's face. He breaks down, a lost brother weeping in full view of his found brothers. Sending his Egyptian attendants away, he unmasks himself, revealing his brother-identity: "I am Joseph your brother, whom you sold in Egypt." (45:4). Then, by returning good for evil, he goes on to teach them a great lesson in the meaning of brotherhood . He reframes their unbrotherly act by saying, "It was not you that sent me here, but God." (45:8) Joseph cries and hugs his brother Benjamin, who weeps with him in return. The moment is then repeated with each brother in turn. Just as it did for Esau and Jacob, the brothers' weeping and kissing each other restores a sense of brotherhood torn apart by envy and injustice.

Psychology of Scarcity vs Psychology of Surplus

Hasidism makes a fundamental distinction between two types of personal relationship, one governed by *heshbon,* a "tit for tat" type of scorekeeping or personal accounting, the other governed by *hesed,* loving kindness in which one acts with unreasonable generosity. To do to a sister or a brother only as s/he has done to you is to live in the world of *heshbon.* To return good for bad is to do *hesed.* The danger of the world of *heshbon* is an endless cycle of retaliation; the danger of the world of *hesed* is vulnerability to victimization. The benefits of *heshbon* are "knowing the score," returning good for good, and bad for bad, as in the optimal strategy for resolving the Prisoner's Dilemma: "Do unto others as they have done to you."[55] The benefits of *hesed* include the fact that the slate is always clean: you never have to keep score.

This "kissing-weeping reunion" of brothers is the moment when *heshbon* is transformed into *hesed.* Joseph and his brothers, weeping together, come to realize what it means to have lost and then found a brother. Joseph regains his sense of brotherhood and becomes his brothers' keeper. His example gives a new twist to the children's rhyme "finders, keepers; losers, weepers" which now becomes "sisters, keepers; brothers, weepers."

After Joseph reveals himself, he gives each brother presents, but to Benjamin he gives a much larger share, "three hundred pieces-of-silver and five changes of clothes." (45: 22) In so doing he recreates the original situation in which the favored younger brother receives more than his elder brothers. Why? Ramban, the great biblical commentator, suggests he did so to see if his brothers had genuinely repented.[56] In Judaism, true repentance entails not only remorse but also acting differently in the same situation. Faced again with inequality, the brothers overcome their envy, proving themselves worthy brethren.

In one sense the reunion of the twelve brothers resolves the brother violence that began with Cain and Abel. Brother murder at the beginning and restoration of brotherhood at the end unify the Book of Genesis.[57] Even so, tensions remain. Joseph retains real power over his brothers, who are totally dependent upon him. It is very difficult to develop a genuine sense of brotherhood when one brother is so powerful. One keen observer has noted: "Every exercise of power incorporates a faint, almost imperceptible, element of contempt for those over whom the power is exercised." [58]

Such a one-sided dependency easily leads to mistrust and resentment, and this mistrust erupts immediately after the death of Jacob, when Joseph's brothers said: "What if Joseph holds a grudge against us and repays, yes, repays us for all the ill that we caused him!" (50:5) The brothers appear to be projecting their guilty conscience onto Joseph. They still perceive the relationship in terms of power and *heshbon*. They do not really believe that Joseph has forgiven them; perhaps they have not forgiven themselves. In terms of sibling psychology, there has been a reconciliation, but there is not true brotherhood and forgiveness. They send a fake testimonial from their father begging Joseph to forgive his brothers. (49:17) Hearing this plea, Joseph weeps one last time and then reassures them:

Do not be afraid; is it for me to put myself in God's place?
The evil you planned to do me has by God's design been turned to
good, that he might bring about, as indeed he has, the deliverance
of a numerous people.
So you need not be afraid; I myself will provide for you and

your dependents. In this way, he reassured them with words that touched their hearts.
(50:19–21, JB)

The brothers are still in the tit-for-tat world of *heshbon,* but Joseph, the victim, having transcended his pain and desire for revenge, dwells in the world of *hesed.*

What is striking is that the resolution of the sibling conflict depends upon how the victim responds to his brothers' aggression. This principle is illustrated in the ancient Mesopotamian story of the gods Dumuzi and Enkimdu.[59] Fighting over a woman, these brotherlike figures are brought to the brink of violence when Dumuzi provokes Enkimdu at the riverside. Had Enkimdu responded aggressively, the situation would quickly have accelerated into an endless cycle of violence. The danger is averted, however, when Enkimdu, the victim, unexpectedly deflects the initial provocation and rejects the role of insulted victim. In a clearheaded way he reframes the conflict into a win/win solution. Had he responded from the world of *heshbon,* a cycle of victimizing violence would have begun, a cycle exceedingly difficult to end. In such deadly quarrels, only the victim, working from the world of *hesed,* is in a position to stop the cycle.

The story of Joseph and his brothers represents one resolution of the Cain-Abel dynamic. Although Joseph, the victim, transcends revenge and his role as victim, he stops short of a return to full brotherhood. But Genesis offers one more sibling twist. When Jacob is dying, Joseph brings his two sons, Manasseh and Ephraim, for their blessing. Joseph expects that Manasseh, the elder son, will receive the blessing of the firstborn, but Jacob, the old trickster, crosses his hands and blesses the younger Ephraim with his right hand. When Joseph notices Jacob's "mistake," he tries to correct it, but Jacob replies: "I know, my son, I know—he [Manasseh] too will be a people, he too will be great, yet his younger brother will be greater than he." Thus he made Ephraim go before Manasseh." (48:16–20) In one sense Jacob is only repeating his own story, repeating the tradition of reversing birth hierarchy, of dethronement. But Jewish tradition sees the event differently.

Despite the fact that Manasseh is dethroned and Ephraim made vulnerable to the Cain-Abel complex, the brothers remain true brothers and friends. Both choose to overcome their potential for conflict and competition. As a result, on Sabbath eve parents traditionally bless their children with the words of Jacob "God make you like Ephraim and Manasseh." (48:20) The brothers' example, the *tikkun* or cosmic repair of the original sin among brothers, shows that despite the injustice of favoritism, brothers can embrace as brothers, and sisters can share through sisterhood. If there is one bold message in the Joseph story, it is that however dire things may appear between sisters and brothers, the improbable possibility for a deep sibling repair (*tikkun akhim*) remains.

CHAPTER 6

The Unexpected Brothers: Moses and Job

I think, am sure, a brother's love exceeds
All the world's loves in its unworldliness.
Robert Browning, "A Blot in the 'Scutcheon:
   A Tragedy," *The Works of Robert Browning*, 282.

Moses as a Second Cain

In this chapter I want to focus on extraordinary sibling stories of two biblical figures not usually considered in their sibling context. They are Moses and Job. Moses is a super-successful baby brother, whose very survival is based on the plucky initiative of his parentified older sister-savior, whom the Midrash identified as Miriam. In terms of family dynamics, a "parentified" child is one forced into looking after a younger sibling like a parent, often at the expense of being a child herself. Moses' sister assumes parentlike responsibility for her helpless baby brother. Under the influence of the Laius Complex (the unconscious urge of parents to harm their children), Pharaoh has decreed that all male babies be strangled at birth by their attending midwife. Moses' mother gives birth secretly and hides the child for three months. In desperation she then places her son in a "little-ark of papyrus . . . in the reeds by the shore of the Nile. And his sister stationed herself far off, to know what would be done to him." (Exod. 2:3–4) Without this older sister looking out for him, baby Moses might never have survived. When Pharaoh's disobedient, if compassionate, daughter finds Moses, Miriam quickly arrives and offers to find a nursing woman "from the Hebrews for you, that she may nurse the child for you." (Exod. 2:7) Thus Miriam, the big sister, reunites her baby brother with their mother as both biological and surrogate wet nurse. Miriam, the protective big sister, is the principal influence in this phase of Moses' life, but thereafter, reared in the royal palace, he is cut off from his true sisters and brothers.

When Moses becomes an adult, he leaves the royal palace to discover his lost "brothers" in what might well be considered the most significant example of "sibling nostalgia" in history. In the "field," he sees the burdens and injustices borne by his clan brothers, and then, when he sees "an Egyptian man striking a Hebrew man, (one) of his brothers," (Exod. 2:11) he impulsively strikes down the cruel taskmaster. The killing is explicitly "brother-related." The next day, Moses goes out again among his brothers. When he tries to stop two Hebrew men fighting, one says to him, "Do you mean to kill me as you killed the Egyptian?" (Exod. 2:14) Realizing that the murder has become public knowledge, Moses becomes frightened and flees to the east.

At this point, Moses is like a second Cain. Like Cain he kills out of an inner sense of injustice; like Cain he tries to conceal his murderous deed; like Cain, when his violent deed becomes known to a Great Father, he goes alone into exile. Arriving in Midian, he begins a new life as a political exile, far from his brothers and sisters. While he is in exile, his life history begins to resemble that of Joseph. Like Joseph he marries a local woman; like Joseph he becomes successful; like Joseph he gives his firstborn a name to commemorate his exile: "He called his name Gershom: for he said, I have been a stranger in a strange land." (Exod. 2:22, KJ) Like Joseph he tries to create a life for himself without sisters or brothers.

After many years, a new pharaoh takes control of Egypt. He brutally oppresses the children of Israel, whose cries rise up like the voices of Abel's blood. Then, at the burning bush, Moses receives the call to return to Egypt to deliver his sisters and brothers from their suffering. Moses, however, resists the role of national redeemer. Again and again he presents reasons why he should not go. He is not worthy: "Who am I that I should go to Pharaoh, that I should bring the Children of Israel out of Egypt?" (Exod. 3:11) He does not know what name to call

Him: "I will come to the Children of Israel and I will say to them: The God of your fathers has sent me to you, and they will say to me: what is his name?—what shall I say to them?" (Exod. 3:13) The Israelites will not believe him to be a true prophet: "They will not trust me, and will not hearken to my voice, indeed, they will say: YHWH has not been seen by you." (Exod. 4:1) He is a poor public speaker: "Please, my Lord, no man of words am I, not from yesterday, not from the day-before, not (even) since you have spoken to your servant for heavy of mouth and heavy of tongue am I!" (Exod. 4:10) Finally he pleads that the Lord find somebody else: "Please, O Lord, make someone else Your agent." (Exod. 4:13, JPS) How does God finally convince Moses to take up his calling? I find it remarkable. He convinces Moses by promising him that he will meet his brother: "Is there not Aaron your brother, the Levite—I know that he can speak, yes can speak well, and here, he is even going out to meet you; when he sees you, he will rejoice in his heart." (Exod. 4:14–16) Only when Moses knows he will meet Aaron and be accepted by his brother does he agree to set forth. It is the promise of a brotherly reunion that launches Moses on his career. The two brothers meet and kiss "at the mountain of God." (Exod. 4:27) Their brotherhood is all the more remarkable because they did not grow up together, did not see each other for decades, but still feel a profound brother feeling. Together they return to Egypt. Working in unison they fight injustice, change history, and lead their people to a new destination and a new destiny. Together these reunited brothers create an egalitarian sibling community, the children of Israel. Aaron and Moses lead the people to freedom, with their sister Miriam leading the singing and dancing. Overturning the fate of the First Brothers, these brothers, with their sister, provide a new model for how brothers and sisters can work together to effect transformation and miracles.

In this famous partnership we see the ultimate resolution of the problem of brother violence. Instead of polarized identities, the sibling roles are *complementary*. Moses is an introverted stutterer, Aaron an extroverted orator. Moses is the savvy political leader, Aaron the sanctifying High Priest. Moses is the logos-based lawgiver, Aaron the eros-minded peacemaker. Strikingly, on the one occasion when

Moses and Aaron are physically separated (when Moses goes alone to Mt. Sinai to receive the Torah), a double catastrophe occurs.

Aaron, giving in to popular demand, creates a gold image of God in the shape of a calf. And Moses, when he sees the idol, smashes the Tablets of the Law in an impulsive rage and forces the Children of Israel to drink the golden calf ground up as powder in water. When Moses asks his brother to account for this great sin, Aaron takes no responsibility: "Let not my lord's anger flare up! You yourself know this people, how-set-on-evil it is." (Exod. 32:22) Significantly, Aaron suffers no consequences for his actions. Moses displaces his rage onto the idol worshippers, calling for his clan brothers, the Levites, to rally round and "kill every-man his brother." (Exod. 2:27)

I believe a partnership in contemporary Israeli politics parallels that of Moses and Aaron. For a long time, Ytizhak Rabin and Shimon Peres were bitter rivals. Rabin was a chain-smoking, security-minded general. Peres, a behind-the-scenes diplomat's diplomat, had never served in the military. Nevertheless, during the Middle East peace process they uniquely complemented each other, achieve together what neither could have achieved alone. Despite being adversaries, they formed an extraordinary partnership that led to a peace agreement with the Palestinians—and to the Nobel Peace Prize. When Rabin was assassinated, Peres was unable to maintain the momentum toward peace with justice.

Successful sibling partnerships can be truly outstanding. Think how the varied skills of the Marx brothers created a new genre for comedy and how the Gershwin brothers and, in a different genre, the Bee Gees, collaborated to create some of the most memorable songs of the twentieth century. The Wright brothers made unique contributions to aviation, the Kennedy brothers to American politics. In sports the Williams sisters (in tennis) and the Manning brothers (American football) pushed each other to ever-higher levels of performance.

> *Creative and destructive tensions [are] inherent in the*
> *sister-brother relationship.*
> Lara Newton, *Brothers and Sisters*, xi

Moses, Aaron, and Miriam form an ideal sibling group at the time of the Exodus to freedom. But in the lives of brothers and sisters, conflict necessarily emerges from the shadow. Whenever one sister or brother speaks with the inner authority of the Self, tensions between sibling equality and sibling hierarchy are inevitable. Recall that Moses, like Zeus and King David, rose from the bottom of the family to seize the top job. *In the Desert* (as Numbers is known in Hebrew) reports Aaron and Miriam's challenge to Moses' exclusive style of leadership. They question his unique right to speak in the name of God: "Is it only, solely through Moses that YHWH speaks? Is it not also through us that he speaks?" (Num. 12:2). Scripture "explains" the background of this sibling conflict as "on account of the Cushite wife that he had taken-in-marriage." (Num. 12:1) Research suggests that spouses significantly influence relations among sisters and brothers, for better or worse, and can strengthen or undermine their marriages.[1] A possessive husband or wife, for example, can easily drive a wedge between even the most devoted of siblings, forcing the spouse to choose between a sibling and him/her—as seems to occur here. Moses does not react to this "sibling betrayal," but God's wrath is unmistakable. Descending upon all three siblings in a pillar of cloud, he says it is only Moses to whom he speaks "mouth-to-mouth." When the cloud rises, Miriam is stricken with a leprous skin condition (Num. 12:10). Aaron, surprisingly, escapes punishment once again.

On the other hand, Miriam and Aaron get off easy as compared with their tribal cousins, the family of Korah, who earlier had challenged Moses' rule as authoritarian. The priests of Korah, along with their wives and children, were swallowed down into the earth. (Num. 16:1–33) Brother Aaron, admitting his guilt and accepting Moses' status as head of the sibling hierarchy, asks forgiveness for their sister: "Let her not be as one dead who emerges from his mother's womb with half his flesh eaten away." (Num. 12:12, JPS) Aaron's evocation of their common womb is effective. Following Moses's prayer (the shortest and most effective in all scripture), "O God, pray, heal her, pray" (Num. 12:13), Miriam is quickly healed. In this way, Moses, the wounding brother, becomes his sister's healing keeper.

Brothers and Sisters in the Book of Job

There is one more sister/brother story in the Bible that I want to discuss. Strangely enough it is in a place rarely associated with brothers and sisters, namely the *Book of Job*. In the opening of the story, Job's seven sons and three daughters seem an ideal sibling group. Taking turns, the brothers feast at each other's house, inviting their three sisters to join them. Job, in sharp contrast to his celebrating, carefree children, is an anxious parent: "Perhaps my children have sinned and blasphemed God in their thoughts." (Job 1:5–6, JPS). No explanation is given for Job's anxiety; he might meet the criteria for a diagnosis of anxiety disorder. Instead of receiving analysis or medication, however, Job makes special sacrifices for their imagined sins. There is no obvious clue to the cause of Job's anxiety, but it is possible that he was picking up some unconscious feelings from his children, as an analyst does using what Michael Fordham called, "syntonic countertransference." Regardless, his worst fears come true when all ten children are killed while feasting at their eldest brother's house.

In *Answer to Job,* Jung asked an important question regarding the meaning of Job's sufferings. Was Job changed by his suffering? I believe so. The evidence is in his sibling experience. Toward the end of the book, Job's previously absent brothers and sisters appear suddenly and unexpectedly, and they "console and comfort him for all the misfortune that the Lord had brought upon him." (Job 42:11, JPS). Acting as ritual siblings, they give Job what his four "friends" failed miserably to provide. They all eat together, and Job's siblings give him ceremonial mourning gifts, restoring the sense of community that Job had lost in the depth of his grief. As Benjamin Disraeli wrote: "Sweet is the voice of a sister in the season of sorrow."[2]

Job has ten more children born to him. His reconstituted family is reminiscent of those Holocaust survivors who lost and recreated their murdered families. Once again he has seven sons and three daughters. What has changed? No change is recorded in connection with his sons. But a dramatic change occurs in his relationship with his daughters. Previously his daughters were nameless. Now each is given a warm and special individual name: Jemimah, Keziah, Keren-happuch. The personal names emphasize their individuality and Job's individuated relationship with each of them. They are praised for their beauty: "Throughout the land there were no women as beautiful as the daughters of Job." (Job 42:15, JB) I understand this statement as reflecting how Job perceived his daughters. Most significantly, they are given inheritance rights equal to their brothers'. Job's suffering seems to have changed his relationship to the feminine and to his own daughters, his sons' sisters.

Now I can offer an interpretation of Job's anxiety at the beginning of the story. Previously, I suggest, Job unconsciously experienced his daughters' resentment at being dependent on their brothers—as Joseph's brothers resented their dependence on him. These sisters had no right to complain openly; indeed they might not have been fully conscious of their own resentments. Living by the rules of patriarchal society, the sisters had received "generous," if patronizing, treatment from their brothers. Nevertheless, they must have felt the fundamental unfairness of such gender discrimination. It is this unconscious hostility and the ever-present danger that it will be acted out as "sin" that Job might have sensed by means of his parental syntonic countertransference. If this interpretation is plausible, then Job's giving estates to his daughters resolves this secret envy among the siblings, closing the circle of envy that began with Cain. Perhaps that is the hidden meaning in this statement: "The Lord blessed the latter years of Job's life more than the former." (Job 42: 12, JPS)

Brothers and Sisters: Clinical Implications

Because sibling relationships are rarely talked about in any depth, most of us grope for words to describe our emotions; about brothers and sisters we are strangely inarticulate. I have never met a person who would not want to improve a stale or hurtful or confusing relationship with a sibling.
Stephen Bank, coauthor, with M. Kahn, of *The Sibling Bond*, xi.

Like the ability to speak, cry, or respond to a baby's smile, so too, the ability to be a brother or sister is innate, part of what Jung called, "the constantly-repeated experience of humanity."[1] The innate nature of the brother-sister bond is illustrated by a fascinating interpretation of the biblical story of creation of man and woman discussed in chapter 1.

Each of us has the potential to be every single kind of sibling—older brother or younger sister; solo, twin, or triplet; half brother or stepsister—but our unique family constellation allows us to experience only one of the myriad sibling possibilities. Jung was perhaps the first psychologist to discuss the stages of life from the perspective of depth psychology. Going through the life cycle often helps us understand the experience of significant others. Falling in love and being married allows us to understand our masculine and feminine, our anima and animus. Becoming a parent usually forces us to evaluate our own mother or father from a new perspective. But the life cycle rarely provides a natural opportunity for us to understand our own brother's or sister's very different experience. The "sibling challenge" of clinical work is to understand the brotherly and sisterly experience of people whose birth orders differ dramatically from our own. To help stimulate this skill, I want to try another active imagination.

Active Imagination 2

The goal of this active imagination is to understand in depth a birth order different from your own. Choose either your brother or sister, the one with whom you have least connection, or a birth position that may not even exist in your family. If you are a firstborn, imagine being the middle child, always caught in between. If you are the sandwich child of the family, imagine being the youngest and never having to grow up. If you are the "baby," imagine being the pioneering eldest, doing everything first while everyone watches you. If you are an only child, imagine having an identical twin and never being alone. If you're a twin, imagine living life solo, never sure whom you can let in. Take a moment and allow images and feelings to emerge.

Then imagine each of the other sibling positions in your family and other sibling positions most foreign to you.

I believe this exercise is important for therapists who must understand the depth psychology of sibling experiences very different from their own.

Understanding Another's Birthright

As I studied the subject of birth order, I searched professional and humanistic literature for material about how a brother or a sister sought to understand the experience of a sibling. What I discovered was that almost no authors sought to explore their brothers' or sisters' experience or to understand what it meant to be their brother or their sister. I did find some convincing exceptions. Nat Bennett provides a rare example of thinking "what it must be like to be my younger brother:"

What must it be like . . . to have an older brother who judges your every effort and exceeds you in some important way no matter what you accomplish? How would it feel to be forever running after someone who expects you to be as smart, as skeptical, and as sad as he is? What do you do if you are born too late to compete, if you love someone more than they can properly requite, if you realize the object of your worship is, in some fundamental way, a fraud? . . . It is very hard to be the younger brother of a brilliantly sardonic tortured-artist type who never quite makes good. . . .

I'm sure being my little brother is not always a picnic.[2]

Another example comes from the Tamil version of the Indian epic *Ramayana,* which was discussed in chapter 3. Rama, the hero of *Ramayana,* has given up his kingdom and set off into the forest with his bride, Sita, and brother, Lakshmana. While in the forest, before Sita is kidnapped, Lakshmana builds a beautiful hut for Rama and his bride, a gesture that moves Rama to tears. Rama recalls that when he left the kingdom, Lakshmana tried to convince him to rebel against his father and seize the kingdom. Because a father's word is sacred, Rama dismissed the idea as madness. Although he is sure he did the right thing, Rama suddenly realizes how his decision affected his brother:

People will say of me that I followed my father's command
when he gave away the rich kingdom—that I did what was
right
and was crowned with fame brighter than the sun. And so
what?
What's it worth when I caused you
such sorrow?[3]

Rama, the older brother, suddenly has a penetrating, transformative, understanding of his younger brother's experience.

I believe that understanding unfamiliar brother and sister roles is the major sibling challenge in clinical work with wounded brothers and suffering sisters. With this renewed ability to imagine the lives of our siblings, I want to turn to clinical matters.

Sibling Transference

"Transference" usually refers to feelings, derived from important parental figures, that are "transferred" to the therapist in the course of treatment. But in reality, as Mario Jacoby noted, "transference exists in all close relationships—transference in the sense that we unconsciously experience the other person as an object for our own needs."[4] "Sibling transference" occurs when a person transfers the emotional aspects of the brother/sister relationship to a person who symbolically resembles that sibling. The birth order of the analyst, something almost never disclosed, may also have a profound impact. If you are a therapist or analyst, how does your birth order affect your clinical work? Think of the patient you most connect with. What is his/her birth order? Think of the patient you love to hate. What is his/hers? Now imagine you meet a patient who has a terrible relationship with a sister named Judy, the name of your own sister with whom you also have a rocky relationship. Finally, imagine treating a patient who closely resembles that sibling you find most difficult.

Sibling transference is not limited to the consulting room but may occur anywhere. A positive sibling transference makes it easy to form and maintain family-like attachments with strangers, especially when the setting symbolically replicates a harmonious family environment. Coleman believed that all working alliance in therapy is based upon a positive sibling transference.[5] Agger suggested that solo children often form sibling attachments to their therapist as the brother or sister they never had.[6] Sibling issues may be especially relevant in working with individuals who suffer from eating disorders.[7] The issues may well play a protective role by mitigating the effects of divorce, trauma, and separation.

In contrast, the hallmark of negative sibling transference is a recurrent tendency to engage in rivalry and hierarchy disputes—who is first, and who got more. Classroom situations easily make "siblings" of classmates who face a shared Parent-Teacher. If the teacher has a "pet," intense sibling transference is almost inevitable. At other times, sibling transference can be marked by ambivalence, as for example in the love-hate relationship so common among brothers and sisters. Freud himself described such a sibling transference, which he confessed was based on his relationship with his nephew John, with whom he grew up during the first three years of his life and who was one year older. Freud wrote:

> Until the end of my third year we had been inseparable; we had loved each other and fought each other, and . . . this childhood relationship . . . had a determining influence on all my subsequent relations with contemporaries. Since that time my nephew John has had many reincarnations. . . . All my friends have in a certain sense been reincarnations of the first figure. . . . My emotional life has always insisted that I should have an intimate friend and a hated enemy. I have always been able to provide myself afresh with both, and it has not infrequently happened that the ideal situation of childhood has been so completely reproduced that friend and enemy have come together in a single individual.[8]

Freud's sibling transference, seeing comrades as intimate friends or hated enemies, no doubt played itself out in his relationship with Jung, who started as an intimate friend, but ended as the hated brother.

A patient may also be concerned with "therapeutic siblings," such as the analyst's other patients. When positive, transference can create a powerful sibling bond among a therapist's real or imagined patients; when negative, transference can create interminable envy, in which therapeutic space is spoiled by the fact that others have entered it. Lesser claimed that neglect of feelings rooted in sibling relationships may be a common source of therapeutic stalemate or failure.[9] Prophecy Coles describes how understanding just such a sister transference provided a key insight which broke open a therapeutic impasse:

> I had become stuck for a very long time in a therapy with a female patient, Mrs. K. She would repeat an endless litany of her

sins and I could make no inroads into her impacted superego. One day she mentioned her elder sister in a way that helped me to grasp that we had been locked into a transference enactment, in which I was this hated sister. . . . She had experienced me much the same way as she had experienced her bossy elder sister, and I had not been aware of this possibility.[10]

Coles then adds that until that moment she had never thought about a sister transference, nor had she read about it. One survey found that although almost none of the therapists received any training in working with sibling transferences, all reported experiencing sibling issues in their work.[11] Coles's short volume, *The Importance of Sibling Relationships in Psychoanalysis*, tried to make the case for a paradigm shift. She argues more generally that very harsh superegos are a hallmark of actual sibling cruelty.

The situation is most intense in psychoanalytic training institutes. There, candidates inevitably seem to carry a sibling imprint. In my training group, for example, candidates often bonded, like sisters and brothers, forming a lasting sense of solidarity. I still feel close to the people I trained with, especially those with whom I shared my analyst. In less favorable emotional circumstances, candidates might compete ruthlessly for attention and approval from seminar leaders and supervisors.

Cain Complex and Abel Complex

Previously I discussed sibling dynamics between Abel and his brother. In this section, I want to link that biblical account to a clinical vignette in terms of Cain complex and Abel complex.

Cain Complex

A person experiencing a "Cain complex"[12] is chronically given to intense feelings of envy and interminable social comparisons in which s/he feels "unchosen." Murray Stein has drawn a psychological portrait of the inner life of these individuals. They are subtly identified as rejected children, as the "bad" sons or daughters. Often they are older children displaced in the affections of parents by younger children. They have "great difficulty forming and maintaining relationships" and live "in a world of continuous vulnerability to envy reaction." Such tormented individuals feel alienated from Self. They lack a comfortable inner center, but instead experience a void that is filled only occasionally and then by tormenting self-accusations. They "cannot soothe themselves . . . cannot find comfort in meditation or active imagination. . . . [They] mostly experience anxiety, low self-esteem, emptiness and critical inner voices. If another figure does appear in this person's active imagination or fantasy, it becomes the object of envy; it is the preferred one, the favored, the chosen. . . . The person [experiencing the Cain complex] . . . is thrown back into feelings of rejection and worthlessness . . . of being abused and shamed . . . a soul in hell, consigned to everlasting torment by an indifferent or hostile parent/God."[13]

In treatment, the central task is to make envy conscious, but treating victims of chronic envy is not easy. Often the use of empathy only makes matters worse: "Soothing analytic words can exacerbate pain . . . since the patient knows the analyst prefers other patients. . . . [The] patient comes in at the end of a long line of preferred others. The transference is heavily loaded with expectations of rejection and humiliation. The analyst can become an object of envy. . . . Someone else always has more of the Self."[14] The patient identifies with the outcast child who has been condemned and driven into isolation. In isolation the patient feels worthless, filled with envy toward favored ones. Consumed by hatred and a desire to destroy, s/he feels evil. The aggressive urge does not necessarily result in homicide but in "murder turned inward," in which suicide may be contemplated as "an act of generosity and goodness to diminish the presence of evil in the world." Suffering from a Cain complex is indeed a curse: there is no inner place of rest, only ceaseless, restless, homeless envy.

Cain's envy represents an extreme sibling position. Cain, the victim of original sibling sin, tried to blot out his brother. Most siblings, of course, do not literally kill each other, but they might harbor murderous feelings and "kill" their siblings symbolically. Symbolic killing may involve wounding the sibling every time they meet. Alternatively, the envious sibling might harden his/her heart, cut off all contact, or refuse to speak.

Let me tell the story of two sisters whom I shall call Cheryl and Joyce. Cheryl, the elder sister, grew up with a Cain-like sense of injustice at having been dethroned by Joyce, the younger, whom Cheryl perceived as both more beautiful and better at school. Joyce was considered easy-going, clever, and lovable. The displaced Cheryl was often irritable. As adults they, like Leah and Rachel, were further polarized by marital and fertility status. Cheryl was divorced, childless, and bitter, but looked after their aged mother with extraordinary devotion. Joyce, too, had divorced, but she had remarried and now was happily married with children. She lived far away and, preoccupied with her growing family and career, visited her mother and sister rarely. Although she was better off financially, she contributed little financially to her mother's care. This unequal burden of caring for an elderly parent is not unusual. In most families, one child does the great majority of parent care.

Cheryl paid for the bulk of her mother's expenses with the understanding that she would be subsequently compensated from her mother's estate. When the mother died, however, the will divided her assets equally between the sisters. Cheryl, having done so much for her mother, was deeply hurt, indeed enraged, at the perceived injustice. Joyce, on the other hand, thought it only fair to divide things equally. Consequently, when the sisters tried to speak, they fought. Cheryl walked out and then cut off all contact with Joyce and her family. The following year, when Cheryl became seriously ill, she forbade relatives from telling her sister. Joyce did not learn about her sister's death until months after the funeral.

The roots of Cheryl's Cain complex were passed down from her mother, who was not on speaking terms with one of her own sisters. Such emotional cutoffs run in families. By caring for her mother, Cheryl had a hidden agenda: undoing the dethronement and becoming the favorite child of her mother, who, for Cheryl, still carried the imprint of the Self. The will was a public humiliation because it deprived her of the special status she had acquired as her mother's caregiver. For Cheryl, an equal share was less than she deserved. In the end, she symbolically killed Joyce by saying, " I have no sister."

Abel Complex

As a parallel to the Cain complex, I believe, one can also speak of an "Abel complex." Individuals suffering from an Abel complex feel favored but always at someone else's expense. Typically this "preference at a price" begins with siblings, but subsequently it can be experienced almost anywhere as a part of a "sibling transference." Unlike the "angel child" who gloats over his/her "devil siblings,"[15] a sibling with an "Abel complex" feels an overwhelming sense of guilt at the inequality from which s/he benefits. Such a person is deeply wounded in his/her capacity to receive, because every "gift" is experienced as a deprivation of an Other. These individuals are trapped in a personal psychology characterized by emotional scarcity: there is never enough to go around. In compensation, such individuals may even develop an exquisite sense of social justice, akin to what my mentor, Robert Jay Lifton, called "animating guilt."[16] They may transfer the Abel complex from the family of origin into the society as a whole, arguing that no one should receive unless all receive equally. As a result, like Mahatma Gandhi or Martin Luther King Jr. (neither of whom were firstborns!), they may be capable of enormous acts of altruism and personal renunciation, as contributors to, or even founders of, altruistic or egalitarian movements.

If, however, such individuals cannot link up with a symbolic brotherhood or sisterhood, they often are left with a static or self-lacerating feeling of guilt and unworthiness based on their unconscious identification with their rejected sibling. Those weighed down by an Abel Complex experience their sibling's unconscious hostility even when the rejected sibling does not express it overtly. They can never wholeheartedly enjoy their successes, because they feel forever that their "brother" or "sister" is watching. They yearn for a psychology of surplus but feel condemned to live within a psychology of scarcity. They cannot free themselves from Cain's haunting question, "Am I my brother's watcher?"

A clinical vignette may help illustrate aspects of the sibling psychology of the Abel complex. The man I shall call "Samuel"[17] was, like his biblical namesake, a person who "grew in esteem and favor both with God and men." (1 Sam. 2:26, JPS) He was married and had two teenage sons when a severe midlife crisis brought him to his knees and into analysis. Despite all his outward success, he had a profound sense of being unworthy, with a tendency to self-blame. He was very concerned with issues of social and environmental justice. He found it easy to give to others but very difficult to receive in return—characteristic of the Abel complex.

During the remodeling of his home, he became upset because of an incident involving his two sons that was reminiscent of the dispute between Cain and Abel. The remodeling was to provide his sons new, separate quarters downstairs, with the parents remaining upstairs. Originally the boys had shared a room, but the younger son, wanting his own space, had moved into Samuel's compact downstairs office. In the new arrangement, one room was larger but with a low ceiling, the other smaller but with a high ceiling. The elder son was given first choice of rooms. Samuel rationalized this preference by saying that the elder was giving up a bigger room. Family friends, he recalled, had argued the reverse: the younger brother, who had a smaller room, should get first choice. As a father, Samuel acutely experienced the wounds of his firstborn, who was unable to give verbal expression to his inner wounded feelings of dethronement.

Initially the elder brother chose the smaller room with the high ceiling. As the renovations continued, however, he had second thoughts, undoubtedly helped by the taunting of his younger brother: "I'm getting the bigger room! I'm getting the bigger room!" He said he wanted to reserve his final decision until he could see the finished rooms. He said that he needed to feel at home in the new space, that judging by the room dimensions alone, he found it hard to tell how just how he would feel. The younger brother reacted vehemently: "You already chose, and you cannot take it back!" A ferocious and seemingly intractable argument ensued. Samuel, caught between his sons, tried to get them to stop, but the brothers continued fighting with enormous hostility and without the hint of a solution. As soon as he could, Samuel went off to be by himself and began crying uncontrollably.

In analysis, Samuel's sadness brought into focus his childhood relations with his own elder brother. They too had fought, to the extent that they had drawn an imaginary line down the middle of the room that each was forbidden to cross. When he was young, he had been nicknamed "Me, too!" He would say this every time his brother received a treat. On the one hand, it indicated an idealization of his brother—"I want what he gets." On the other, it showed that he felt he could easily be left out and forgotten. Unkept and unseen, Samuel's Abel complex was only heightened when some years later a younger sister was born, changing him from a younger brother to a middle child. Furthermore, this sister was a special-needs child to whom Samuel's mother devoted extraordinary efforts. Again Samuel was neglected and this time with no right to complain.

His older brother could never stand up to their powerful, judgmental father. Reacting to his brother's negative experience, Samuel developed a defensive persona that he called "Mr. Contrary." Whatever position his father would take on any issue, Samuel would take the opposite. Without any personal investment in the debate, he could argue passionately, expressing the resentment both brothers felt toward this distant, judgmental authority figure. His older brother admired Samuel for his courage, but Samuel knew he could be strong only if the issue was one he really didn't care about—and he hardly knew what he really cared about. As a result he felt he was a fraud, an imposter. An inner voice would continually accuse him, saying, "If only they knew the real truth about you."

Samuel felt there must have been something earlier to create such inner mistrust and not allow himself to feel good about himself. The memory that eventually emerged was an image of an early sibling Oedipal triangle. Samuel saw himself as an infant at his mother's breast while his brother, only fourteen months older was screaming. Never when he nursed, looking into his mother's distracted eyes, did he feel that he had her full attention. Mother's milk carried the sibling imprint of his brother's screaming. Everything he received thereafter was scarred by a sense that it came at someone else's expense.

My empathy and identification with Samuel might well have been influenced by my own sibling countertransference. As I will soon explain, I am also a younger brother of an older brother. Although I did not develop a full-blown Abel complex, I did feel guilt and unease at receiving praise when he did not. In working with Samuel, I believe I was able to make use of my own experience as a "wounded brother" to help provide healing and deeper insight into his sibling situation. Elsewhere I have described how a chance encounter led to a breakthrough in Samuel's treatment. There I discussed how the encounter outside analysis strengthened therapeutic container to a higher level of psychic security, which I called "temenos regained." Now I believe that the turning point also can be understood within brother transference. Samuel had made good and steady progress in analysis, but I felt that something was missing. To tell the truth, I was thinking in Freudian terms, of a repressed memory. With synchronicity, around that time, I met Samuel by chance at the opening of a public event. We greeted each other, and then I quietly left. At the next session he asked why I had left the event. I explained what had guided my behavior. My desire was to protect the temenos, to do nothing that might endanger our work together. I could see he was very moved by what I had said, especially by the fact that I had done something against my personal interest for his benefit. He said no one had done that for him before, and then he left.

When he returned for his next session, he told me what was missing. It was not a repressed memory but something he had consciously withheld. It was a bitter experience that had haunted him for years, especially on the Hebrew Day of Atonement, Yom Kippur, when Jews traditionally confront their sins. He revealed that he had yearned to tell me on many previous occasions, from the beginning, but never found the right moment. And then he told me his secret: he had been used as a sex toy by a neighbor, something for which he had always blamed himself. I recall how he flinched when I said he had been sexually abused. "But I agreed!" he cried out. "You were a child," I answered, "and you needed protection." His tears were the beginning of a healing journey.

In retrospect, I believe Samuel experienced me as a caring older brother he never had who was looking out for him. The transference experience let him begin to develop a caring inner brother. The interplay between "inner siblings" and "outer siblings," both personal and archetypal, is surely worthy of further exploration.

Resolving Polarized Identity

Earlier I argued that to live within the framework of polarized identities is to live in a fragmentated world. How does one heal such a world? One simple approach I find effective in working with polarized siblings is to transform an outer shadow sibling into accessible inner sibling. When an individual faces a difficult situation that brings out an inferior side, I often ask, "How would your sister, or brother, cope with this situation?" Let me give a brief example. A free-spirited, if somewhat disorganized, artistic sister, Helen, was polarized with her successful accountant brother, Paul, who was neat and logical but emotionally constricted. As a result, Helen looked down on Paul as compulsive, and Paul looked down on her as chaotic. Each sibling experienced the other's territory as "off limits." In working on their polarized relationship, Helen came to understand that Paul had many valuable capabilities she lacked, traits that actually helped one survive in the world. Activating the brother within allowed her to discover hidden logos skills. For the first time she developed a filing system for her papers and got her income-tax forms in on time. Synchronistically, Helen's inner changes changed something in Paul. Suddenly able to access a previously hidden creativity, he took up charcoal drawing, no doubt helped by the sister within. Integrating a shadow sibling often unfreezes a stuck sibling relationship, as it did for Paul and Helen. Now they had more to talk about than ever before, and naturally they felt closer than ever. Resolving polarized identity may also allow each sibling access to other sibling niches from which s/he previously felt cut off. In this way sibling development might hold a key to the individuation process itself.

I believe that analytical psychology will be profoundly enriched by exploring the role of sibling archetype and sibling dynamics in the work of healing. Brothers and sisters play an important role in mythology and archetypal imagery, in metaphors and social life, in family life and the development of the personal, in sibling transference and countertransference, and more. I believe that the study of the role of siblings in psychotherapy and analysis is "the new psychoanalytic frontier."[18] Is it not time that we Jungians return to our roots and rediscover the significance of brothers and sisters?

Afterword: A Personal Note

*That is what it means to have brothers and sisters, I
suppose, in the last analysis: there is no ice to break.*
Kelsh and Quindlen, *Siblings*, 110.

I want to conclude with a personal note about my own experience as a
brother. I have an older brother, Lavy, and an older sister, Ilana, making me the "baby" of the family. My parents stopped giving Hebrew
names when it came to me, and perhaps in some strange way, that is
why I am the only one who came to live in Israel. All of us were born
in the short space of three years, nine months. My parents married
late and were, I suppose, making up for lost time. As a result, we were
extremely high access siblings. I had intensely close relations with
each of my siblings, but for reasons not clear to me, that was not true
of them. They were planned; I was not. With my sister, I always had
a natural togetherness. A year and a half apart in age, but only a year
apart in school, we shared a secret language, special adventures, and
a vision of life to be lived to the full. We both wrote poetry and acted
in theatricals. (Ilana, an early star, performed semi-professionally in
"Children's Theater.") To this day, at a moment's notice, we can reenact old, familiar sketches from theater days, *The Three Stooges*, old TV
shows, or bits from *The Importance of Being Earnest*. Each can play-
fully "annihilate" the other with the micromovement of an eyebrow
and can do imitations of teachers from high school. Overall, the relationship was, and is, warm and harmonious.

There were tensions, of course, but most were subsumed in a playful camaraderie, or at least that is my perception. When my own chil-

dren were young, I saw glimpses of our childhood when my daughter would run hand-in-hand with her younger brother. My sister was beautiful, full of vitality, and sensitive, but she had difficulty finding her "intended" one. I wondered if our special connection somehow interfered with her ability to find a loving partner. At times I felt I had to back off. Eventually, at age sixty, she found a truly wonderful life partner and married.

I came into a world in which siblings occupied a natural place. My brother, the firstborn, did not. In an attempt to spare him the "trauma" of dethronement, my mother rather unnaturally gave him extra attention to protect him from the rejection he nevertheless felt. His special treatment compromised the legitimacy of his underlying displeasure and his emotional freedom to express it.

When we both were younger I often felt that he played a much greater role in my psychic life than I did in his. We shared a room, but really it was his. He had his own desk; I used the dining-room table. On at least one occasion he exiled me from "our room," angrily placing all my possessions outside in the hall. Lavy was temperamentally private: introverted, sensitive, shying away from conflict or company. I was outgoing, sociable, easygoing, loveable. Our identities were polarized, and he was a bad psychological match to our much more outgoing, expansive, often overpowering mother. He was considered the "difficult" child; I, the easy one. I think he took out his various frustrations on me, periodically beating me up with murderous rage, with and without provocation. Only later did I come to appreciate how difficult his position was. You see, he could never really win. If he asserted his superior strength and really hurt me, I could go crying to Mama. I was the "baby," and he would be chastised. If, on the other hand, he did not fully dominate me, it was a moral victory for me. I was happiest with a draw.

Our father was wonderful with us when we were toddlers. Even now, when he is in his nineties, his eyes light up at the sight of a cute two- or three-year-old. But as we grew up he withdrew into the world of work. My brother felt abandoned by the most important male in his life. I had Lavy, but he had nobody. All this fueled his resentments and led to further beatings.

I looked up to Lavy as a guide and role model, but he deeply resented the burden of being the "wise older brother." To get his attention I developed a neurotic habit of "inadvertently" bumping into him as we walked down the street. Each time he would become annoyed and I would apologize profusely . . . until the next time. As we all know, negative attention is better than no attention, and negative attention I certainly received. Then, when my brother started high school, he told me he wouldn't have time to beat me up anymore. And he didn't. The "murder" was gone, but what remained was a far cry from togetherness.

Later, when Lavy left home to go to graduate school, I would visit him periodically in his new surroundings. I still looked up to him, but I still competed with him about finding "The Truth" or some meaningful spiritual direction. Each visit began with warmth and good intentions, but somewhere in the middle, inevitably, we would have a big fight. Finally, after we had repeated this cycle a number of times, he asked, "What do you want from me?" To my reply, that I needed to be sure he really cared about me, he said, "I cannot imagine anything that would make me stop caring about you, even if maybe you killed somebody." Now I ponder his choice of words, but then I was reassured.

This inner security sustained me during many years when I felt that I was the only one investing in our relationship. Somewhere, even if he didn't show it, I knew he cared. He was always promising to answer that letter or send a birthday gift, but he rarely got around to it. When we met in person, things were fine. But when we separated, I felt again and again how much more he meant to me than I meant to him, and how I was doing the job of both brothers. Things might have continued this way indefinitely—good when we met, not much connection when we didn't—but the coming of email changed everything. My brother is inhibited by a blank page, no doubt a residual trauma from school days. But because he is technically adept and because email allows an easier, more informal pace, we correspond over the ether as we never could in print, and now we both sustain a brotherly friendship of openness and caring.

Like the brothers of Genesis I have passed from murderous feelings to embracing togetherness. Now I am blessed not only with a
sister who is truly like a sister but also with a brother who is truly like
a brother. The opening line of Psalm 133, "How good and pleasant
it for brothers and sisters to live together in peace,"[1] forms one of
the most beloved communal songs in the Hebrew tradition. When
we sing these words, arms intertwined, shoulder-to-shoulder, swaying
back and forth in time to the melody, we enjoy a wonderful moment
of togetherness, a vision of how a world of brotherhood and sisterhood might be. Living together in peace. To paraphrase Martin Luther King Jr., "We must live together as brothers and sisters or perish
together as fools."[2]

Notes

Foreword

1. In the Tao everything comes from the Mother. See Lao Tsu, *The Tao Te Ching: A New English Version*, Stephen Mitchell, trans. (New York: Harper-Collins, 1989).

Preface

1. For a touching account of the role imaginary sisters can play in a person's life, see Angela Pneuman's essay "Sister" in Elisa Albert, ed., *Freud's Blind Spot: 23 Original Essays on Cherished, Estranged, Lost, Hurtful, Hopeful, Complicated Siblings* (New York: Free Press, 2010), 237–42.
2. See Genesis 12:11–13 and 20:2 and for Isaac, 26:7.
3. Everett Fox, trans., *The Five Books of Moses* (New York: Schocken Books, 1995), ix–x.
4. For my version of this split, see H. Abramovitch, "Rabban Gamliel and Rabbi Yehoshua in the Analytic Training Institute: A Talmudic Text (Berachot 27b–28a) and the Group Life of Analysts," at <u>http://www.henry-a.com/apage/110348.php</u>.

Chapter 1

Epigraph: Robert A. Paul, *Moses and Civilization: The Meaning behind Freud's Myth* (New Haven, CT: Yale University Press, 1966), 11.
Epigraph: Elisa Albert, ed., *Freud's Blind Spot: 23 Original Essays on Cherished, Estranged, Lost, Hurtful, Hopeful, Complicated Siblings* (New York: Free Press, 2010), 76.
Epigraph: Albert, *Freud's Blind Spot*, 1.

1. The exceptions are Abraham's threatening to kill his son Isaac and Reuben's sleeping with Bilhah, his father's handmaiden, mother of his half-brothers. Noah and his son Ham are discussed below.

2.   A number of Jungians have published important material on aspects of brother-sister psychology: Christine Downing, *Psyche's Sisters: Re-Imagining the Meaning of Sisterhood* (Dallas, TX: Spring Journal, 2007), and Lara Newton, *Brothers and Sisters: Discovering the Psychology of Companionship* (Dallas, TX: Spring Journal, 2007). The most innovative works are Kristina Schellinski's "Life after Death: The Replacement Child's Search for Self," in Lyn Cowan, ed., *Barcelona 2004: Edges of Experience: Memory and Emergence. Proceedings of the 16th Annual International IAAP Congress for Analytical Psychology* (Einsiedeln, Switzerland: Daimon Verlag, 2006), and Lisbeth von Benedek's *Frére et Soeurs pour la Vie: L'empreinte de la Fraterie sur nos Relations Adultes* (Paris: Eyrolles, 2013). Other important works using the psychodynamic approach include M. D. Kahn and K. G. Lewis, *Siblings in Therapy: Life Span and Clinical Issues* (New York: Norton, 1988), which uses a life-cycle approach; Vamik D. Volkan and Gabriele Ast, *Siblings in the Unconscious and Psychopathology: Womb Fantasies, Claustrophobia, Fear of Pregnancy, Murderous Rage, Animal Symbolism, Christmas and Easter "Neuroses," and Twinnings or Identifications with Sisters and Brothers* (Madison, CT: International Universities Press., 1997), which examines unconscious representation of siblings in a traditional psychoanalytic framework; and Leon Ainsfeld and Arnold D. Richards, *The Replacement Child: Variations on a Theme of History and Psychoanalysis* (New Haven, CT: Yale University Press, 2000). For an overview, see Ruth S. Eissler, Albert J. Solnit, and Peter B. Neubauer, eds., *The Psychoanalytic Study of the Child*, vol. 38 (New Haven, CT: Yale University Press, 1983), especially A. B. Colonna and L. M. Newman, "The Psychoanalytic Literature on Siblings." Prophecy Coles, *The Importance of Sibling Relationships in Psychoanalysis* (London: Karnac Books, 2003), is a recent overview. S. A. Sharpe and A. D. Rosenblatt, "Oedipal Sibling Triangles," in *Journal of American Psychoanalysis Association* 42:491–523, reinterprets Oedipal triangles in terms of sibling relationships. And Juliet Mitchell, *Siblings: Sex and Violence* (London: Polity Press, 2004), argues for the centrality of sibling relationships. All these studies comment on the neglect of sibling issues.

3.   Charles W. Nuckolls, ed., *Siblings in South Asia: Brothers and Sisters in Cultural Context* (New York: Guilford Press, 1993), 3.

4.   Nuckolls, *Siblings in South Asia*, 31.

5.   See Taylor Clark, "Plight of the Little Emperors," *Psychology Today*, 2008, http://www.psychologytoday.com/articles/200806/plight-the-little-emperors

6.   S. Bank and M. Kahn, *The Sibling Bond* (New York: Basic Books, 1982).

7. Walter Toman reported that the best marriages were between individuals
    of different birth orders, especially if they had siblings of the opposite sex
    (e.g., older brother with younger sisters marrying a younger sister with
    older brothers or vice versa). Higher rates of marital discord and divorce
    were found when marriage partners had the same birth order or had no
    siblings of the opposite sex. The marriages of solo children were particular-
    ly prone to difficulties. See Walter Toman, *Family Constellation: Its Effects
    on Personality and Social Behavior*, 4th ed. (New York: Springer Publishing,
    1992). Toman's results remain controversial.

8. George E. Vaillant and Caroline O. Vaillant, "Natural History of Male
    Psychological Health, 12: A Forty-Five-Year Study of the Predictors of Suc-
    cessful Aging at Age Sixty-Five," *American Journal of Psychiatry* 147:31–37.

9. Katharine Hepburn, *Me: Stories of My Life* (Penguin: London, 1991), 16.

10. Coles, *The Importance of Sibling Relationships in Psychoanalysis*.

11. Sigmund Freud, *Case Histories 1: Dora and Little Hans*, vol. 8 in *The Pen-
    guin Freud Library*, James Strachey and Angela Richards, eds. (New York:
    Penguin, 1977), 167–305.

12. Virginia M. Axline, *Dibs: In Search of Self* (New York: Ballantine Books,
    1973).

13. D. W. Winnicott, *The Piggle: An Account of the Psychoanalytic Treatment of
    a Little Girl* (London: Hogarth Press, 1978).

14. Sigmund Freud, *The Standard Edition of the Complete Psychological Works
    of Sigmund Freud*, vol. 17, *An Infantile Neurosis and Other Works* (London:
    The Hogarth Press and the Institute of Psycho-analysis, 1918), 156.

15. Ernest Jones, *Sigmund Freud: A Life and Work*, vol. 1 (London: Hogarth
    Press, 1953).

16. Sigmund Freud, *Introductory Lectures on Psychoanalysis*, vol. 15 in *The
    Standard Edition of the Complete Psychological Works of Sigmund Freud*
    (London: The Hogarth Press and the Institute of Psycho-analysis,
    1915–16), 153. Freud's baby brother, Julius, died on March 15, 1858. Seven
    months later, on December 31, a baby sister, Anna, was born. At the same
    time, Sigmund's beloved nanny, Resi, "turned out to be a thief." Freud's
    half-brother, Philip, "went himself to fetch the policeman, and she got ten
    months." (P. C. Vitz, *Sigmund Freud's Christian Unconscious* [New York:
    Guilford Press, 1988], 114). The unconscious association of the loss of the
    nanny and the birth of a sister likely influenced his emotional attitude to
    the many closely spaced siblings that followed, eight in a period of only ten
    years. For a fuller discussion of Freud's relation to his siblings, see Bank
    and Kahn, *The Sibling Bond*.

17. Sigmund Freud, *The Origins of Psychoanalysis: Letters to Wilhelm Fleiss, Drafts and Notes 1897–1902*, M. Bonaparte, A. Freud, and E. Kris, eds. (New York: Basic Books, 1959), 219.

18. In *Totem and Taboo and Other Works*, vol. 13 of *The Standard Edition of the Complete Psychological Works of Sigmund Freud*, Freud did discuss a "just so" story in which brothers are unified by their joint murder of an authoritarian patriarch. This "fantasy" generated much controversy but had little or no clinical impact. Robert Paul (*Moses and Civilization: The Meaning Behind Freud's Myth* [New Haven, CT, Yale University Press, 1996]) provides an updated if apologetic discussion of "Totem and Taboo." He argues that Freud's primal horde most resembles a gorilla family, in which one dominant male controls a harem of females while unattached males await their chance to displace him.

19. Carl Jung and Aniela Jaffé. *C. G. Jung: Memories, Dreams, Reflections*, Richard Winton and Clara Winton, trans. (New York: Pantheon Books, 1963), 25.

20. Jung and Jaffé, *C. J. Jung*, 25.

21. C. G. Jung, *The Complete Works of C. G. Jung*, Gerhard Adler, ed., R. F. C. Hull, trans., vol. 17, *Development of Personality* (Princeton, NJ: Princeton University Press, 1954), para. 7.

22. Jung and Jaffé, *C. J. Jung*, 112.

23. Jung and Jaffé, *C. J. Jung*, 112.

24. Francine Klagsburn, *Mixed Feelings: Love, Hate, Rivalry, and Reconciliation among Brothers and Sisters* (New York: Bantam Books, 1992), xii.

25. Siegel, Rosalie, personal communication, 2003.

26. T. H. Ogden, *The Primitive Edge of Experience* (Northvale, NJ: Jason Aronson, 1989), 95.

27. Winnicott, *The Piggle*, 161.

28. Winnicott, *The Piggle*, 177.

29. See especially the work of Judy Dunn and her associates in J. Dunn, C. Kendrick, and R. MacNamee, "The Reaction of First-born Children to the Birth of a Sibling: Mothers' Reports," *Journal of Child Psychology and Psychiatry* 22:1–18; J. Dunn and C. Kendrick, *Siblings: Love, Envy and Understanding* (Cambridge, MA, Harvard University Press, 1982); Judy Dunn, *Sisters and Brothers: The Developing Child* (Cambridge, MA, Harvard University Press, 1985); and J. Dunn, "Psychology of Sibling Relations," in N. J. Smelser and P. B. Baltes, eds., *International Encyclopedia of the Social and Behavioral Sciences* (Oxford, Pergamon, 2001), 14063–66.

30. Melanie Klein, *Love, Guilt, and Reparation and Other Works 1921–1945*,

vol. 1 in *The Writings of Melanie Klein*, Roger Money-Kyrle, ed. (London: Hogarth Press, 1975).

31. Klein, *Love, Guilt, and Reparation.*

32. Mitchell, *Siblings*, 114.

33. Grosskurth, *Melanie Klein: Her Work and Her World* (London, Maresfield Library, 1985), 13.

34. Grosskurth, *Melanie Klein*, 62.

35. Grosskurth, *Melanie Klein*, 39.

36. Melanie Klein, "The Sexual Activities of Children," in *The Psychoanalysis of Children*, vol. 2 in *The Writings of Melanie Klein*, Roger Money-Kyrle, ed. (London, Hogarth Press, 1975), 118–19.

37. George A. Barton, *Archaeology and the Bible*, 3rd ed. (Philadelphia: American Sunday School, 1920), 413–16.

38. *Midrash Rabbah*, H. Freedman and Maurice Simon, trans., vols. 1–3, *Genesis* (London: Soncino Press, 1939), 3:6.

39. For more on royal brother-sister incest marriage, see Ray H. Bixler, "Sibling Incest in the Royal Families of Egypt, Peru and Hawaii," *Journal of Sex Research* 18:264–81.

40. *New English Translation of the Septuagint and Other Greek Translations Traditionally Included under That Title* (NETS) (Oxford: Oxford University Press, 2007).

41. In 1 Chronicles 2:9, Tamar is especially singled out: "All were David's sons, besides the sons of the concubines; and Tamar was their sister."

42. For more on negative effects of sibling sex abuse, see John V. Caffaro and Allison Conn-Caffaro, *Sibling Abuse Trauma: Assessment and Intervention Strategies for Children, Families and Adults* (New York: Haworth Press, 1998).

Epigraph: C. G. Jung, *The Collected Works of C. G. Jung*, Gerhard Adler, ed., R. F. C. Hull, trans., vol. 9, part 2, *Aion: Researches into the Phenomenology of the Self* (Princeton, NJ: Princeton University Press, 1969), para. 126.

43. C. G. Jung, *The Collected Works of C. G. Jung*, Gerhard Adler, ed., R. F. C. Hull, trans., vol. 11, *Psychology and Religion: West and East* (Princeton, NJ: Princeton University Press, 1970), para. 629.

44. Emmanuel Kennedy, personal communication, 2004.

45. See Brian Sutton-Smith and B. G. Rosenberg, *The Sibling* (New York: Holt, Rinehart & Winston, 1970). In this pioneering study, Sutton-Smith and Rosenberg developed a shorthand notation for indicating the place of a sibling within the overall birth and gender order. According to this notation, Moses, the third child, following an eldest sister and middle brother,

would be represented as "FMM3." The birth order is listed by the number, the gender by letter. The scheme, however, has not caught on. Consequently there is no widely accepted way of describing sibling sequence and birth order.

46. Edward F. Edinger, *Ego and Archetype: Individuation and the Religious Function of the Psyche* (Boston, MA: Shambhala Publications, 1973), 36.

47. See *The Analytic Encounter* (Toronto: Inner City Books, 1984).

48. John Beebe, "The Case of Joan: A Classical Perspective," in Polly Young-Eisendrath and Terence Dawson, eds., *The Cambridge Companion to Jung* (Cambridge University Press, 1997), 196.

Chapter 2

Epigraph: Douglas W. Mock and Geoffrey A. Parker, *The Evolution of Sibling Rivalry* (Oxford: Oxford University Press, 1977), 411.

1. According to Douglas W. Mock and Geoffrey A. Parker, in *The Evolution of Sibling Rivalry* (Oxford: Oxford University Press, 1997), 88, "Siblicide is well documented in many species of predatory birds, arctic fox, Galapagos seal and spotted hyena, who practice sororicide." See also Dereck Joubert and Beverly Joubert, *Eternal Enemies: Lions and Hyenas.* National Geographic Video, 1998. On the other hand, altruistic behavior is even more apparent among siblings in many species.

2. Nick Kelsh and Anna Quindlen, *Siblings* (New York: Penguin Studio, 1998), 9–10.

3. Kelsh and Quindlen, *Siblings,* 15–16.

4. Deborah, T. Gold, "Sibling Relations in Old Age: A Typology," *International Journal of Aging and Human Development* 28:37–51.

5. S. Bank and M. Kahn, *The Sibling Bond* (New York: Basic Books, 1982), 84ff.

6. Benjamin Tammuz, "My Brother," in *Six Israeli Novellas.* Gershon Shaked, ed. (Boston, MA: David R. Godine, 1999), 219, 267, 284–85.

7. Helen Exley, *Brothers! Quotations Selected by Helen Exley* (New York: Helen Exley Giftbooks, 1996), 18.

Epigraph: Nick Kelsh and Anna Quindlen, *Siblings* (New York: Penguin Studio, 1998), 37.

8. This question is the title of the influential article by Robert Plomin and Denise Daniels in *Behavioral and Brain Sciences* 10:1–60.

9. Frank J. Sulloway, *Born to Rebel: Birth Order, Family Dynamics, and Creative Lives* (New York: Pantheon Books, 1996), 70.

10. Alfred Adler, *Understanding Human Nature* (New York: Permabooks 1949).

11. Thomas Moore, *Care of the Soul* (London: Piatkus, 1995), 80.

12. Helen Brammer-Savlov, "Brother/Sister Archetype: Images of Contrasexual Sibling Bonds." Unpublished qualification thesis, Independent Group of Analytical Psychologists, London 2004. Thanks to Helen Brammer-Savlov for making her thesis available to me.

13. See R. Blanchard and A. F. Bogaert, "Homosexuality in Men and Number of Older Brothers," *American Journal of Psychiatry* 153:27–31.

14. For research on the impact of gender order on the personality of younger siblings, see J. Dunn, "Psychology of Sibling Relations," in *International Encyclopedia of the Social and Behavioral Sciences*, N. J. Smelser and Paul B. Baltes, eds. (Oxford: Pergamon 2001), 14036–66.

Chapter 3

Epigraph: Ricardo J. Quinones, *The Changes of Cain: Violence and the Lost Brother in the Cain and Abel Literature* (Princeton, NJ: Princeton University Press, 1991), 7.

1. P. Lal, trans., *Mahabharata of Vyasa* (Glen Oaks, NY: Asia Book Corporation of America, 1970), 57.

2. Yudisthera almost certainly would meet contemporary criteria for a diagnosis of pathological gambling. On page 295 of their *Concise Textbook of Clinical Psychiatry* (Baltimore, MD: Williams & Wilkins, 1997), H. I. Kaplan and B. J. Sadock characterize pathological gambling as "a preoccupation with gambling; the need to gamble with increasing amounts of money to achieve the desired excitement; repeated unsuccessful attempts to control, cut back, or stop gambling; gambling as a way of escaping from problems; gambling to recoup loses; lying to conceal the extent of the involvement with gambling; the commission of illegal acts to finance gambling; the jeopardizing or loss of personal and vocational relationships because of gambling; and a reliance on others for money to pay off debts."

3. P. Lal, *Mahabharata of Vyasa*, 71.

4. Sophocles, *Antigone*, 908–13.

Chapter 4

Epigraph: Frederick E. Greenspahn, *When Brothers Dwell Together: The Preeminence of Younger Siblings in the Hebrew Bible* (New York: Oxford University Press, 1994), 4.

1. Jacob Licht, *Storytelling in the Bible* (Jerusalem: Magnes Press, 1986), 32.

2. For more on active imagination, see Joan Chodorow, *Jung on Active Imagination* (Princeton, NJ: Princeton University Press, 1997).

3. For an introduction to the Midrash, see Reuven Hammer, *The Classic Midrash: Tannaitic Commentaries on the Bible* (Mahwah, NJ: Paulist Press, 1995) and Jacob Neusner, *The Midrash: An Introduction* (Northvale, NJ: Jason Aaronson, 1994). For treatment of the genre in the context of modern literary criticism, see Geoffrey Hartman and Sanford Budick, eds., *Midrash and Literature* (New Haven, CT: Yale University Press), 1986. The most accessible collection of Midrash in English is Louis Ginzberg *The Legends of the Jews* (Jewish Publication Society of America, 1909), a continuous narrative of diverse legendary material available in a seven-volume edition that includes scholarly notes (1969) and in a condensed two-volume version (2003). The largest single collection is available in a ten-volume edition, *Midrash Rabbah: Genesis*, H. Freeman and Maurice Simon, trans. (London: Soncino Press, 1939).

    A reliable source on Midrash concerning Genesis 4 is Noam Zion *On the Origins of Human Violence: An Introduction to the Midrash Agada; The Story of Cain and Abel* (Jerusalem: Shalom Hartman Institute, 1994). A scholarly German source is Viktor Aptowitzer, *Kain und Abel in der Agada den Apokryphen, der hellenistichen, cristlichen und muhammedanischen Literatur* (Vienna: R. Lowitt Verlag, 1922).

    Some questions addressed in the Midrash concerning the story of Cain and Abel are: How were the two brothers born? Why do they have different professions? How did the Lord pay heed to one offering and not to the other? What did Cain say to Abel in the field? What did they quarrel about? How did brother kill brother? Did Cain really intend to murder Abel, or was it an accidental homicide? Given that Abel's death is the first in scripture, did Cain know what death was? Why did Cain receive mercy and not the judgment meted out to subsequent murderers? What was the mark of Cain? Where did Cain find a wife? How should murderers be punished? Did Cain repent? What kind of wandering did he do? How did he die?

4. Irving Harris, *The Promised Seed: A Comparative Study of First and Later Sons* (New York: Free Press, 1964).

5. Howard Cooper, "Persecution and Silence: The Myth of Cain and Abel," *Harvest* 33:12.

6. Examples of "brother-referential" naming are found in various biblical genealogies. The sons of Eber are described in this manner: "Two sons were

born to Eber: the name of the first was Peleg/Splitting, for in his days the earth-folk were split up; his brother's name was Yoktan. (10:25) Similarly, the sons of Nahor, Abraham's brother, are named: "Uts, the first born, and Buz, his brother." (22:20) The genealogies in Chronicles contain many examples of brothers listed in birth order. David is listed as seventh in birth order in his family of origin, along with his two sisters, Zeruiah and Abigail. David's six sons born to him in Hebron are listed in birth order. Likewise, in the genealogy of the tribe of Benjamin it is written that the sons of Eshek were "Ulam his first born, Jehush the second, and Eliphe-let the third. (1 Chronicles 8:38–9, JPS) Brother-referential genealogy contrasts with strict patrilineal identity, in which only the first born or heir in each generation is named. There are 629 references to "brother(s)" and 114 to "sister(s)" in the Old Testament. (Avraham Even-Shoshan, *A New Concordance of the Bible: Thesaurus of the Language of the Bible, Hebrew and Aramaic Roots, Words, Proper Names Phrases and Synonyms* (Chicago: Board of Jewish Education, 1984)

7. In *A Commentary on the Book of Genesis*, Part 1 (I. Abrahams, trans. [Jerusalem: Magnes Press, 1964), Umberto Cassuto noted that many words in Genesis 3–4 recur as multiples of seven: "Abel," "earth" (*'erets*), "name," and "field" each occur seven times; "Cain" and adama, fourteen times; Eden, east, and garden, twenty-one times; and the Divine Name, thirty-five times. At the seventieth mention of the Divine Name in Genesis, it is written, "At that time they first called out the name of YHWH." (4:26)

8. Albert, *Freud's Blind Spot*, 3.

9. Benjamin Tammuz, "My Brother," *Six Israeli Novellas*, Gershon Shaked, ed. (Boston, MA: David R. Godine, 1999), 284–85.

10. *Midrash Rabbah*, H. Freedman and Maurice Simon, trans., vols. 1–3. *Genesis* (London: Soncino Press, 1939), 22:2.

11. S. Bank and M. Kahn, *The Sibling Bond* (New York: Basic Books, 1982).

12. Ron Hansen, "The Story of Cain," in *Genesis as It Is Written: Contemporary Writers on Our First Stories*, David Rosenberg, ed. (San Francisco: Harper, 1996), 51.

13. Asch, Sholem. *In the Beginning: Stories from the Bible* (New York: Schocken Books 1969), 12–3, based on Midrash Bereshit Rabbah 22:7.

14. Research on the tactics ten-year-olds employ to get their siblings to do what they want indicates that eldest children typically use high-powered tactics and younger siblings build alliances. (Brian Sutton-Smith and B. G. Rosenberg, *The Sibling* [New York: Holt, Rinehart & Winston, 1970])

15. Cassuto (1964) compared genealogies in 10:1 and 10:2, in 11:27 and
    11:27–28, and in 25:9 and 25:12. In all three the eminence order is given
    first, the literal birth order second.

16. O. D. Edwards, "Druids, Priests, Bards, and Other Fathers." In *Fatherhood:
    Men Writing about Fathering.* S. French, ed. (London: Virago, 1992), 69.

17. *Midrash Rabbah, Genesis,* 2:5.

18. Michael Dorris, "The Story of Abel," in *Genesis as It Is Written: Contem-
    porary Writers on Our First Stories,* David Rosenberg, ed. (San Francisco:
    Harper, 1996), 49–50.

19. In *Text and Texture: Close Readings of Selected Biblical Texts* (New York:
    Schocken Books, 1979), Michael Fishbane follows Ibn Ezra and other
    commentators in rejecting a "blame the victim" approach. On page 64 of
    "Why God Rejected Cain's Offering: The Obvious Answer," in *Fortunate the
    Eyes That See: Essays in Honor of David Noel Freeman in Celebration of His
    Seventieth Birthday,* Astrid B. Beck, Andrew H. Bartlett, Paul R. Raabe, and
    Chris A. Franke. eds. (Grand Rapids, MI: Eerdmans, 1995), Gary Herion
    says Cain's offering was rejected because it was from the earth that God
    had cursed. He adds, "Generations of subsequent Israelites would offer
    to God the same sort of agricultural goods that Cain had offered (Lev.
    2:10–16) but in a different era when the curse of the soil had been lifted."
    (Herion, "Why God Rejected Cain's Offering," 64)

20. E. Mavis Hetherington, "Parents, Children and Siblings: Six Years After," in
    Relations within Families. R. A. Hinde and J. Stevenson-Hinde, eds. (Ox-
    ford: Oxford University Press, 1988).

21. Murray Stein, "The Pattern of Envy and Sibling Rivalry in Myth and
    Religion," in *Psyche and Family: Jungian Applications to Family Therapy,* L.
    Dodson and T. Gibson, eds. (Wilmette, IL: Chiron Publications, 1996), 99.

22. Edward F. Edinger, *Ego and Archetype: Individuation and the Religious
    Function of the Psyche* (Boston, MA: Shambhala Publications, 1973), 43–44.

23. Murray A. Straus and Richard J. Gelles, "Societal Change and Change in
    Family Violence from 1975 to 1985 as Revealed by Two National Surveys,"
    Journal of Marriage and Family 48 (3):465–79.

24. Alfred Adler, *Understanding Human Nature* (New York: Permabooks,
    1949), 135.

25. W. R. D. Fairbairn, *Psychoanalytic Studies of Personality: The Object Relation
    Theory of Personality* (London: Routledge & Kegan Paul, 1981).

26. Robert Graves and Raphael Patai, *Hebrew Myths: The Book of Genesis*
    (London: Cassell, 1963) 92.

27. Philip Roth. *The Human Stain* (Boston, MA: HMH Books, 2000), 328.

28.   Diana Baumrind, "The Development of Instrumental Competence through Socialization," in A. Pick, ed., *Minnesota Symposium on Child Psychology* (Minneapolis: University of Minnesota Press, 1973), 3–46.

29.   Frits Boer and Judy Dunn, *Children's Sibling Relationships: Developmental and Clinical Issues* (New York: Psychology Press, 1992), and Francine Klagsburn, *Mixed Feelings: Love, Hate, Rivalry, and Reconciliation among Brothers and Sisters* (New York: Bantam Books, 1992).

30.   J. Jill Suitor, Jori Sechrist, and Karl Pillemer, "When Mothers Have Favorites: Conditions under Which Mothers Differentiate among Their Adult Children," *Canadian Journal on Aging* 26:85–99.

31.   *Babylonian Talmud,* Tractate Yoma 52, accessible at: http://halakhah.com

32.   Joseph Heller, *God Knows* (New York: Alfred A. Knopf, 1984), 288–89.
Epigraph: Dorris, "The Story of Abel," 45.

33.   Juliet Mitchell also notes the link between Genesis 4 and Leviticus 19: "There is a fundamental desire to murder your sibling. It too meets a prohibition: you must not kill your brother Abel; you must instead love your brother (neighbor) *as yourself.* The violence must be turned into love—but the possibility of love is already there in the love one has for oneself, what, in psychoanalytic terminology, is called narcissism." (*Siblings: Sex and Violence* [London: Polity Press, 2004], 35)

34.   Harold Jacobson, *The Very Model of a Man* (New York: Viking, 1992), 318.

35.   See Nahum M. Sarna, *Understanding Genesis* (New York: Jewish Theological Seminary with McGraw-Hill, 1966), 33.

36.   The word for "field" occurs 333 times in scripture, but the phrase "rising up in the field" calls to mind the violent rape described in Deuteronomy: "If *in the field* the man find the spoken-for girl and the man strongly seizes her and lay with her, then he is to die, the man who lay with her, he alone. But to the girl you are not to do anything, the girl did not (incur) sin (deserving) of death, for just as (the case of) the man who *rises up* against his neighbor and murders his life, so is this matter: for *in the open-field* he found her; when the spoken-girl cried out, there was no deliverer for her." (emphasis added)

   Using the passage from Deuteronomy as a reference point for Genesis 4, we can imagine that Abel did cry out in the field but that there was no "deliverer" to hear his cry.

37.   Ricardo J. Quinones, *The Changes of Cain: Violence and the Lost Brother in the Cain and Abel Literature* (Princeton, NJ: Princeton University Press, 1991), 5.

38.   Jacobson, *The Very Model of a Man,* 328.

39. Arthur Miller, "The Story of Adam and Eve." In *Genesis as It Is Written: Contemporary Writers on Our First Stories,* David Rosenberg, ed. (San Francisco: Harper, 1996), 37–38.

40. C. G. Jung, *The Collected Works of C. G. Jung,* Gerhard Adler, ed., R. F. C. Hull, trans., vol. 16, *The Practice of Psychotherapy: Essays on the Psychology of the Transference and Other Subjects* (Princeton, NJ: Princeton University Press, 1966), paras.124–25. According to Jung, the other stages of psychotherapy are: *elucidation,* based on interpretive method and working out of transference relations; *education,* in its literal sense of drawing out; and *transformation,* or *individuation,* in which a person becomes more and more himself and less "normal" or "adapted." See also Andrew Samuels, *Jung and the Post-Jungians* (London, Routledge & Kegan Paul, 1985).

41. F. F. Schachter and R. K. Stone, eds., *Practical Concerns about Siblings: Bridging the Research-Practice Gap* (New York: Haworth Press, 1987).

42. R. B. Felson and N. Russo, "Parental Punishment and Sibling Aggression," *Social Psychology Quarterly* 51:11–18, and G. R. Patterson, "Siblings: Fellow Travelers in Coercive Family Processes," in *Advances in the Study of Aggression,* R. J. Blanchard and D. C. Blanchard, eds. (Orlando, FL: Academic Press, 1984), 173–215.

43. Klagsburn, *Mixed Feelings,* 186.

44. Dan Pagis, "Autobiography," in *The Selected Poetry of Dan Pagis,* Stephen Mitchell, trans. (Berkeley: University of California Press, 1989), 5.

45. There is no ambiguity in the story of Cain and Abel as told in the *Qur'an"*

> Narrate to them exactly the tale of the two sons of Adam. When each of them offered a sacrifice (to God), that of one was accepted, and that of the other was not.
>
> *Said (the one): "I will murder you,"*
> *And the other replied: "God only accepts*
> *From those who are upright and preserve themselves from evil.*
> *If you raise your hand to kill me,*
> *I will not raise my hand to kill you,*
> *For I fear God, the Lord of all the worlds;*
> *I would rather you suffered the punishment*
> *For sinning against me, and for your own sin,*
> *And became an inmate of Hell.*
> *And that is the requital for the unjust."*
> *Then the other was induced by his passion*

To murder his brother, and he killed him,
And became one of the damned.
Ahmed Ali, *Al-Qur'an: A Contemporary Translation*, sura 5:27–32
(Princeton, NJ: Princeton University Press, 1988), 101–102.

From the perspective of victim psychology, Abel's initial response, "I
will not raise my hand," is the kind of unexpected nonretaliatory response
that can stop brother violence. By contrast, his later words, "I would rather
you suffered punishment . . . and became an inmate of Hell," are inflamma-
tory.

46. "My punishment is too great to bear!" is from JPS. Compare JB, KJ, RA,
    MF, SM.

47. Dorris, "The Story of Abel," 43.

48. Dorris, "The Story of Abel," 48.

49. Many traditional Jewish sources support this translation: *Onkelos on the
    Torah: Understanding the Bible Text: Genesis*, Israel Drazin and Stanley M.
    Wagner, trans. (Jerusalem: Gefen Publications, 2006); *Sapirstein Edition
    Rashi, The Torah with Rashi's Commentary*, Rabbi Yisrael Herczeg, trans.,
    vol.1, *Genesis* (*Bereishis*) (Brooklyn, NY: Artscroll/Mesorah Publications,
    1999); Ramban (Nachmanides), *Commentary on the Torah*, 5 vols. (New
    York: Judaica Press, 2005); and sources quoted in James L. Kugel, *Traditions
    of the Bible: A Guide to the Bible as It Was at the Start of the Common Era*
    (Cambridge, Mass: Harvard University Press), 155. For an overview, see
    Ruth Malinkoff, *The Mark of Cain* (Berkeley, University of California Press,
    1981).

50. Ali, *Al-Qur'an*, sura 5:31–32.

51. Martin Buber, *The Knowledge of Man: A Philosophy of the Interhuman*,
    Maurice Friedman, ed. (New York: Harper Torchbooks 1965). On page
    139 of *The Broken Connection: On Death and the Continuity of Life* (New
    York: Simon & Schuster, 1979), Robert Jay Lifton, expands on Buber. He
    identifies "static guilt," a deadening immobilization of the self that can be
    self-lacerating; "numbed guilt," which prevents guilt by "freezing" the self
    and numbing experience in general; and "animating" guilt, an energizing,
    transformative power that leads to renewal and change.

52. *Midrash Rabbah* 22:2.

53. *Midrash Rabbah* 22:13.

54. On the psychological importance of home, see Carl Jung and Aniela Jaffé,
    Memories, Dreams, Reflections (London: Collins, 1963), 250–65; Theodore
    Abt, *Progress without Loss of Soul* (Wilmette, IL: Chiron Publications,

1988), 127–40; and Clare Cooper Marcus, *House as a Mirror of Self: Exploring the Deeper Meaning of Home* (Berkeley, CA: Conari Press, 1997). On the sacred and homelike sense of the therapeutic space, see H. H. Abramovitch, "Temenos Lost: Reflections on Moving," *Journal of Analytical Psychology* 42:69–84, and H. Abramovitch, "Temenos Regained: Reflections on the Absence of the Analyst," *Journal of Analytical Psychology* 47:583–97.

Epigraph: Klagsburn, *Mixed Feelings,* 290. The quote is by a man discussing the murder of his brother.

Epigraph: Yann Martel, *The Life of Pi* (Toronto: Random House, 2001), 141.

55. Abram loses his brother in his native land; Ishmael loses touch with his brother, Isaac; and Jacob flees from Esau, who wishes to kill him. Rachel and Leah flee from their brothers. Shelah witnesses the premature death of both his elder brothers. Simon and Levi are galvanized into action at the presumed loss of their sister Dina. The story of Joseph and his brothers revolves around the presumed death of a brother.

56. Jamaica Kincaid, *My Brother* (New York: Farrar, Straus and Giroux, 1998), 156.

57. Barbara Lazear Ascher, *Landscape without Gravity: A Memoir of Grief* (Harrison, NY: Delphinium Books, 1992), 128. Ascher and Kinkaid each lost an alienated younger brother to AIDS.

58. Martin Buber, *The Knowledge of Man: A Philosophy of the Interhuman.* Maurice Friedman, ed. (New York: Harper Torchbooks, 1965).

59. Dante, naming the icy bottommost ring of Hell "Caina" after Cain, shares the view of Cain's violence as archetypal. A pair of brothers who killed each other are encased in the ice, "packed in head to head, so tightly that their hair was interknit. . . . Each butted the one he faced in helpless rage." A shade says, "They issued from one body, and if you went all over Caina you could not find a shade worthier to be frozen in punishment." (Dante Alighieri, *The Inferno of Dante: A New Verse Translation,* canto 32, Robert Pinsky, trans. [London: Dent, 1997], 343).

  On page 65 of *The Changes of Cain,* Quinones writes: "[Cain] must continue to live as the first victim of the personal terror brought about by the atmosphere of reciprocal violence, the vendetta he helped to introduce. . . . Cain is presented not as the epitome of envy, but rather as the initiator of violence who turns out to be its natural victim, living in dread of retaliation. This is the picture of Cain the terrorized, not Cain the terrible." Quinones' book is an outstanding overview of the theme of Cain and Abel in Western literature.

60. For an excellent and comprehensive discussion of this type of "brother

violence," see Donald L. Horowitz, *The Deadly Ethnic Riot* (Berkeley: University of California Press, 2001).

61. Jostein Gaarder, *Sophie's World: A Novel about the History of Philosophy* (New York: Farrar, Straus, Giroux, 2007), 166.

Chapter 5

Epigraph: Anonymous

1. Frances F. Schachter, Ellen Shore, Susan Feldman-Rotman, Ruth E. Marquis, and Susan Campbell, "Sibling Deidentification." *Developmental Psychology* 12 (5):418–27; Frances F. Schachter, "Sibling Deidentification in the Clinic: Devil vs. Angel." *Family Process* 24 (3):415–27; and F. F. Schachter and R. K. Stone, eds., *Practical Concerns about Siblings: Bridging the Research-Practice Gap*, New York: Haworth Press, 1987.

2. In *The Psychology of the Transference* (Princeton, NJ: Princeton University Press, 1969), Jung describes a fundamental social instinct or emotional force that holds families together and that, by implication, unites communities and nations. On page 62 he calls this special unifying psychic energy "kinship libido:" "Incest, as an endogamous relationship, is an expression of the libido which serves to hold the family together. One could therefore define it as 'kinship libido,' a kind of instinct which, like a sheep-dog, keeps the family group intact." On pages 71 and 72 he describes kinship libido as the primary bonding instinct of social life:

    "There is one connection in the transference which does not break off with the severance of the projection. That is because there is an extremely important instinctive factor behind it: the kinship libido. This has been pushed so far into the background by the unlimited expansion of the exogamous tendency that it can find an outlet, and a modest one at that, only within the immediate family circle, and sometimes not even there, because of the quite justifiable resistance to incest. While exogamy was limited by endogamy, it resulted in a natural organization of society that has entirely disappeared today. Everyone is now a stranger among strangers. Kinship libido—which could still engender a satisfying feeling of belonging together, as for instance in the early Christian communities—has long been deprived of its object. But, being an instinct, it is not to be satisfied by any mere substitute such as a creed, party, nation, or state. It wants the *human* connection. That is the core of the whole transference phenomenon, and it is impossible to argue it away, because relationship to the self is at once relationship to our fellow man, and no one can be related to the latter until he is related to himself."

Kinship libido is the driving force behind family and familiar feeling. It lies at the heart of the sibling bond and the sense of brotherhood and "the human connection." It is the basis of nonbiological or "fictive" kinship, when individuals and families establish a sibling bond not by birth but by choice. The most dramatic fictive kinship involves the literal or symbolic sharing of blood to become "blood brothers" or "blood sisters." These potential siblings are chosen because they seem like a sibling. Some such bonds are secret; others include and obligate families of the blood siblings. Blood brothers and blood sisters are always chosen. Divorce and remarriage, by contrast, create new, often unwanted siblings. Children living in such blended families might discover the older brother or younger sister they have yearned for, but more often they feel no kinship libido with their new, unchosen brothers and sisters. Instead, they are forced to cope with an exogamous stranger with whom they may feel no emotional connection. When young siblings wish to wound one another, they say, "You were adopted!" or, "You were found on the doorstep"—as if to say, "You are not really one of us!" The success of blended families depends largely on the gradual development of kinship libido.

3. Randal Keynes, *Darwin, His Daughter, and Human Evolution* (New York: Riverhead Books, 2001), 237.

Epigraph: Kristina Schellinski, "The Search for Self and Other When Born to Replace Another Human Being," Presentation to the 8th Jungian Odyssey, "Echoes of Silence: Listening to Soul, Self, Other," 18 June 2013.

Epigraph: Carl Gustav Jung, *The Red Book,* Sonu Shamdasami, ed., Sonu Shamdasani, Mark Kyburz, and John Peck, trans. (New York: W. W. Norton, 2009), 296.

4. Translated by Julia Roessler. In Kristina Schellinski, "The Search for Self and Other When Born to Replace Another Human Being," Presentation to the 8th Jungian Odyssey, "Echoes of Silence: Listening to Soul, Self, Other," 18 June 2013. The full text is in Victor Hugo, *Les Contemplations* (Quebec, QC: Librairie Générale Francaise, 1972). See also Kristina Schellinski, "Life after Death: The Replacement Child's Search for Self," in *Barcelona 2004: Edges of Experience: Memory and Emergence, Proceedings of the 16th Annual International IAAP Congress for Analytical Psychology,* Lyn Cowan, ed. (Einsiedeln, Switzerland: Daimon Verlag, 2006), 781.

5. Richard A. Kalish, *Death, Grief, and Caring Relationships* (Monterey, CA: Brooks/Cole, 1985).

6. For a discussion of replacement psychology, see A. C. Cain and B. S. Cain, "On Replacing a Child," *Journal of the American Academy of Child Psychia-*

try 3:443–56; Maurice Porot's insightful "L'enfant de remplacement" (Paris: Frison-Roche, 1993). For a Jungian perspective, see Kristina Schellinski, "'Oh, Brother:' A Jungian Perspective on the Challenges and Opportunities Faced by a Replacement Child," Diploma Thesis, C .G. Jung Institute, Zurich, 2002; Schellinski, "Life after Death: Replacement Child," Presentation at the 2nd European Conference on Analytical Psychology, St. Petersburg, 31 August 2012; Schellinski, "The Search for Self and Other When Born to Replace Another Human Being:" and Helen Brammer-Savlov, "Brother/Sister Archetype: Images of Contrasexual Sibling Bonds." Unpublished diploma thesis, 2004, Independent Group of Analytical Psychologists, London.

7. Schellinski, "'Oh, Brother," and Schellinski, "Replacement Child."

8. Carl Gustav Jung was born July 26, 1875, after his mother Emilie mourned the deaths of three children: a daughter who was stillborn on July 19, 1870, a daughter who was stillborn on April 3, 1872, and a son, Paul (named after his father), who was born on August 18, 1873, but died five days later (Deirdre Bair, *Jung: A Biography* [Boston, MA: Back Bay Books, 2004], 18).

9. Salvador Dali, *The Secret Life of Salvador Dali.* (New York: Dial Press, 1942), 23.

10. Jung, *The Red Book, 308.*

Epigraph: Benjamin Tammuz, "My Brother," 220.

11. Thanks to Kristina Schellinski for this phrase.

12. See *Babylonian Talmud, Tractate:* Sanhedrin, Folio 70a at: http://halakhah .com See also David Goldenberg, "What Did Ham Do to Noah?" in *"The Words of a Wise Man's Mouth Are Gracious": Festschrift Gunter Stemberger,* Mauro Perani, ed. (Berlin: Walter de Gruyter, 2005), 257–65; http://www .sas.upenn.edu/~dmg2/what%20did%20ham%20do.pdf

13. This verse has served to justify ethnic superiority. White supremacists in America's "Deep South" and racist regimes such as the proponents of apartheid in South Africa, used Noah's, and by extension God's, curse to justify segregating the "Children of Ham."

Epigraph: Yann Martel, *The Life of Pi* (New York: Houghton Mifflin Harcourt, 2002), 124.

Epigraph: Jamaica Kinkaid, *My Brother* (New York: Farrar, Straus and Giroux, 1998), 155–56.

Epigraph: Elizabeth De Tiva-Raeburn, *The Empty Room* (New York: Scribners' 2004), 113.

14. D. Flomenhaft "The Forgotten Ones: The Grief Experience of Adult Siblings of WTC Victims." Ph.D. dissertation, New York University, in Joyce

Edward, *The Sibling Relationship: A Force for Growth and Conflict* (Northvale, NJ: Jason Aaronson, 2012), 156.

15. Edward, *The Sibling Relationship*, 156.

16. Abraham's magnanimous gesture raises the issue of his birth-order status. Genesis 11:26 does list him first, but this might reflect "order of eminence" rather than birth order. That the story of his brother Haran is presented before Abraham's indicates that Haran was older. Abraham most likely was a middle child. For a fuller discussion, see Abramovitch, *The First Father. Abraham: The Psychology and Culture of a Spiritual Revolutionary* (Lanham, MD: University Press of America, 1994), 59.

17. J. Dunn and P. Munn, "Development of Justifications in Disputes with Mother and Children," *Developmental Psychology* 23:791–98.

18. Some Hebrew commentators regard Abraham's bargaining with God (Gen.18:17–31) as the action of an "emergency sibling." They suggest that Abraham stopped bargaining at ten just men because he knew that Lot and his family would form at least that number. After Abram rescues Lot, he has fascinating dialogues both with the king of Sodom and with Melchizedek, king of Salem and priest of God Most High, but none with Lot, which suggests that his motivation was more universal than that of an emergency brother.

19. *The Straight Story,* directed by David Lynch, Disney Studios, 1999.

20. For more on 'linking objects' in the mourning process, see Volkan, Vamik D., and Gabriele Ast (1997). *Siblings in the Unconscious and Psychopathology: Womb Fantasies, Claustrophobias, Fear of Pregnancy, Murderous Rage, Animal Symbolism, Christmas and Easter "Neuroses," and Twinnings or Identifications with Sisters and Brothers.* (Madison, CT.: International Universities Press, 1997).

21. The later phrase comes from Helen Brammer-Savlov, "Brother/Sister Archetype: Images of Contrasexual Sibling Bonds." Unpublished thesis, Independent Group of Analytical Psychologists, London, 2004, 42.

Epigraph: Siegel, Rosalie, personal communication describing the dramatic impact of the death of her mother on her relationship with her twin sister: "Suddenly, after my mother died—my father had died long before—the animosity and rivalry evaporated and we are very close and concerned about each other, truly loving and at peace. I have always known that my relationship with my twin was the central psychological element in my life. . . . I would never have guessed in a million years how my relationship to my sister would change after my mother's death, but I certainly understood that once our parents were no longer around that made all the difference in the relationship."

22. Debra Umberton. *Death of a Parent: Transition to a New Adult Identity* (Cambridge: Cambridge University Press, 2006), 188–89.

23. Leonard Kriegel, *Flying Solo: Reimagining Manhood, Courage, and Loss* (Boston, MA: Beacon Press, 1999), 174ff.

Epigraph: Nineteenth-century American humorist Josh Billings.

24. Douglas W. Mock and Geoffrey A. Parker. *The Evolution of Sibling Rivalry* (Oxford: Oxford University Press, 1997). Hi-tech fertility treatments regularly include such intrauterine siblicide. The use of ovulation-stimulating drugs leads to many eggs, and it is standard practice to reduce the number of "ovum siblings" artificially to increase the likelihood that one or two will come to a successful live birth.

   The body sometimes reduces the number of ovum siblings on its own, as when one of two twin fetuses is "reabsorbed" by the body—a process about which little is known. In "chimeraism," a rare phenomenon, the twins fuse into one human being possessing the genetics of both.

Epigraph: Lara Newton, *Brothers and Sisters: Discovering the Psychology of Companionship* (Dallas: Spring Journal, 2007), 43.

25. Laban does bless his sister as she leaves:

> *And they gave Rebekah farewell-blessing and said to her:*
> *Our sister, may you become thousandfold myriads*
> *May your seed inherit the gate of those who hate him! (24:60).*

Compare this with the blessing given to Abraham in 22:17:

> *Indeed, I will bless you, bless you,*
> *I will make your seed many, yes, many,*
> *Like the stars of the heavens and like the sand that is on the shore*
> *   of the sea;*
> *Your seed shall inherit the gate of their enemies.*

26. Robert Barsky, personal communication.

27. For discussions of how parental sibling dynamics are passed onto the next generation, see Josephine R. Hilgard, "Sibling Rivalry and Social Heredity," *Psychiatry* 14:375–85, and S. Bank and M. Kahn, *The Sibling Bond* (New York: Basic Books, 1982).

28. Other translations of the Hebrew term *tam* use "mild man" (JPS), "quiet man" (JB), "simple man" (RA, MF), and "peaceful man" (SM). Noah (6:9) is referred to as *tamim* (a plural form of *tam*) meaning "wholehearted" or

"blameless" (JPS, RA, SM), "a man of integrity" (JB), and "perfect" (MF). In a divine vision, Abraham is commanded: "Walk in my presence! And be wholehearted." (17:1) When the king of Gerar proclaims his innocence (20:5), he uses a similar phrase, '*b'tom levavi,* meaning "with a whole heart," "with a pure heart" (RA), "with a clean conscience" (JB), "with a blameless heart" (SM).

29. Miriam Lichtheim, *Ancient Egyptian Literature,* vol. 2, *The New Kingdom* (Berkeley: University of California Press, 1976).

30. I would like to thank my dear friend Steven Kepnes for illuminating this idea in his paper "Hagar and Esau: From Others to Sisters and Brothers," in Peter Ochs and William Stacy Johnson, eds., *Crisis, Call, and Leadership in the Abrahamic Traditions* (New York: Palgrave Macmillan, 2009), 31–46. As he notes, the face-to-face theme is repeated in 32:31, 33:10, and 33:31.

31. For various another interpretations of Jacob as "Israel," the one who wrestles with God, see Robert Alter, *The Art of Biblical Narrative* (New York: Basic Books, 1981).

32. Everett Fox, trans., *The Five Books of Moses* (New York: Schocken Books, 1995), 32:28–29n.

33. Because Rabbis in the Midrash were ambivalent about Esau's subsequent identity with the Roman Empire, they could not bear to see this first kiss as the sign of brotherly love. Noting that the word for "he kissed him" is "dotted," indicative of a possible scribal error, Rashi (quoting a Breita of Sifrei) claimed that it was a "Judas kiss," not wholehearted—or even that Esau did not kiss him but *bit* him! Rabbi Shimon bar Yochai, however, sees the scene as a precursor of the encounter between Joseph and his brothers: Esau did hate his brother but, when he actually saw him, was overwhelmed and gave him a wholehearted kiss.

Epigraph: Shakespeare, *Henry V*, 4, iii, 60–62.

Epigraph: Jacob's death-bed "blessing" to Shimon and Levi (49:5–7).

34. B. Berelson and G. A. Steiner, *Human Behavior: An Inventory of Scientific Findings* (New York: Harcourt, Brace & World, 1964).

35. For a discussion of "atrocities" in the context of just and unjust wars, see Michael Walzer, "The Triumph of Just War Theory (and the Dangers of Success)," *Social Research* 69 (4):925–44.

36. Fox's translation is less effective: "Should our sister then be treated like a whore?" Alter's rendition works well if it is given an ironic, Yiddish intonation: "Like a whore should our sister be treated?" In a footnote he adds: "This moment becomes the turning point in the story of Jacob. . . . Hence-

forth he will lose much of his paternal power and will be seen repeatedly at the mercy of his sons, more the master of self-dramatizing sorrow than of his own family. This same pattern will be invoked in the David story: the father who fails to take action after the rape of his daughter and then becomes victim of the fratricidal and rebellious impulses of his sons." (Robert Alter, *Genesis: Translation and Commentary* [New York: W.W. Norton, 1996], 194 n. 31).

37. Midrash Rabbah 92:4

Epigraph: Tolstoy, quoted by *Philip D.A. Treffers* "Foreword: Sibling Studies and Sibling Lore" in Boer and Dunn, *Children's Sibling Relationships: Developmental And Clinical Issues*, xi.

Epigraph: Vietnamese proverb.

Epigraph: Nalini Jones, "Who Will Save Us Now?" in Elisa Albert, ed. *Freud's Blind Spot: 23 Original Essays on Cherished, Estranged, Lost, Hurtful, Hopeful, Complicated Siblings* (New York: Free Press, 2010). 102.

38. Ibrahim Muhawi and Sharif Kanaana, *Speak, Bird, Speak Again: Palestinian Arab Folktales* (Berkeley: University of California Press, 1989), 24, 111.

39. Charles Lindholm, *Generosity and Jealousy: The Swat Pukhtun of Northen Pakistan* (New York: Columbia University Press, 1982), 126.

40. Sergei Aksakoff, *Years of Childhood*, J. D. Duff, trans. (New York: Longmans, Green, 1916), in J. Dunn, *Sisters and Brothers: The Developing Child* (Cambridge, MA: Harvard University Press, 1985), 10.

41. Stendhal, quoted in Dunn, *Sisters and Brothers*, 157.

42. Lara Newton, *Brothers and Sisters: Discovering the Psychology of Companionship* (Dallas: Spring Journal, 2007), 1.

Epigraph: Helen Exley, *Sisters!* (New York: Helen Exley Giftbooks, 2008), 29.

Epigraph: T. A. H. McNaron, *The Sister Bond: A Feminist View of a Timeless Connection* (New York: Pergamon Press, 1985), 295.

Epigraph: Albert, *Freud's Blind Spot*, 241.

43. For research on sisters, see Bert, N. Adams, *Kinship in an Urban Setting* (Chicago: Markham, 1968); M. E. Lamb and B. Sutton-Smith, eds., *Sibling Relationships: Their Nature and Significance across the Lifespan* (Hillsdale, NJ: Erlbaum, 1982); Francine Klagsburn, *Mixed Feelings: Love, Hate, Rivalry, and Reconciliation among Brothers and Sisters* (New York: Bantam Books, 1992). For a beautiful photo essay describing the joys of sisterhood, see Carol Saline and Sharon J Wohlmuth, eds., *Sisters* (Philadelphia, PA: Running Press, 2004).

44. Lady Aster, in Exley, *Sisters!*, 20.

45. Angela Pneuman, "Sister," in Albert, *Freud's Blind Spot*, 237.

46. The Hebrew word *duda'im* appears only here and in Song of Songs 7:14. It is traditionally translated as "mandrakes."

47. A strange parallel to these "sexual-sister stories," in which two sisters have sexual relations with a single male, is reported in Judges 15:2. When Samson discovers that his first wife has been married off to one of his wedding companions, his father-in-law offers him her younger sister: "I was sure," said her father, "that you had taken a dislike to her, so I gave her to your wedding companion. But her younger sister is more beautiful than she; let her become your wife instead." Insulted, Samson takes revenge by burning his father-in-law's field and possibly his household.

Epigraph: Modified from Pam Brown, in Exley, *Brothers!*, 43.

48. The traditional translation of the Hebrew *ketonet passim* as "coat of many colors" (KJ, SM) is by no means certain. Alternate translations include "ornamented tunic" (JPS, RA) and "coat with long sleeves" (JB). The only other use of *ketonet passim* is in 2 Samuel 13, where it is said to be worn by virgin princesses, including Tamar, so brutally raped by her brother. As many commentators have noted, that account includes "a whole network of pointed allusions to the Joseph story" (Alter 1996, 209, n.3). Some modern commentators have suggested that the special clothes were a sign that the wearer was heir to his father.

49. For a discussion of biblical dreams and Jewish dream traditions, see Henry Abramovitch, "'The Dream Always Follows the Mouth:' Jewish Approaches to Dreaming," in Erel Shalit and Nancy Swift Furlotti, eds., *The Dream and Its Amplification* (Skiatook, OK: Fisher King Press. 2013), 151–65.

50. C. G. Jung, *The Complete Works of C. G. Jung,* Gerhard Adler, ed., R. F. C. Hull, trans., vol. 7, *Two Essays on Analytical Psychology* (Princeton, NJ: Princeton University Press, 1967), para.78.

51. In M. D. Kahn and K. G. Lewis. *Siblings in Therapy: Life Span and Clinical Issues.* (New York: Norton, 1988), 72.

52. Quoted in W. H. Auden and Louis Kronenberger, eds., *The Viking Book of Aphorisms* (New York: Penguin Books, 1981), 90.

53. Aviva Gottlieb Zornberg, *The Beginning of Desire: Reflections on Genesis* (New York: Schocken Books, 1995), 342.

54. Albert, *Freud's Blind Spot*, 1.

55. The term "Prisoner's Dilemma" derives from game theory. It describes a game in which two confederates in a serious crime are held by the police. The police have no solid evidence against them, but a police detective devises a stratagem to obtain their confessions. Separating the prisoners, he tells each that the other has confessed and that if he too confesses, his sen-

tence will be lessened. But, the detective continues, if he does not confess, the other will turn state's evidence against him, and the prisoner who does not confess will face a long sentence while the other goes free.

If neither prisoner confesses, each will face only a minor charge. Each prisoner's dilemma is whether or not to trust the other. If one thinks the other will confess, it is in his interest to confess as well. If, however, each trusts the other, neither will confess. When the game is played as an isolated event, both prisoners usually confess. When it is ongoing, the best strategy is to repeat what the other prisoner did in the previous round, rewarding cooperation with cooperation and defection with defection. Prisoner's Dilemma provides models in economics, psychology, ecology, animal behavior, and other fields. See Richard Axelrod, *The Evolution of Cooperation* (New York: Basic Books, 1985); Anatol Rapoport., Two-Person *Game Theory* (Mineola, New York: Dover Publications, 1999); and Herbet Gintis, *Game Theory Evolving: A Problem-Centered Introduction to Modeling Strategic Interaction,* 2nd ed. (Princeton, NJ: Princeton University Press, 2009). "Prisoner's Dilemma" is also the title of a play by David Elgar and a novel by Richard Powers.

56. Ramban (Nachmonides), commentary on Genesis 45:22.

57. See Bruce T. Dahlberg, "The Unity of Genesis," K. Gros Louis, ed., *Literary Interpretations of Biblical Narratives,* vol.2 (Nashville, TN: Abingdon, 1982), 126–34, and Dan W. Forsyth, "Sibling Rivalry, Aesthetic Sensibility and Social Structures in Genesis." *Ethos* 19:453–510.

58. Sándor Márai, *Embers,* Carol Brown Janeway, trans. (New York: Vintage, reprint, 2002), 61.

59. See J. B. Pritchard, ed. *Ancient Near Eastern Texts Relating to the Old Testament,* 3rd ed. (Princeton, NJ: Princeton University Press, 1969).

Chapter 6

Epigraph: Robert Browning, "A Blot in the 'Scutcheon: A Tragedy," Act 2, *The Works of Robert Browning* (Ware, Herts: Wordsworth Editions, 1994), 282.

Epigraph: Lara Newton, *Brothers and Sisters: Discovering the Psychology of Companionship* (Dallas: Spring Journal, 2007), xi

1. Francine Klagsburn, *Mixed Feelings: Love, Hate, Rivalry, and Reconciliation among Brothers and Sisters* (New York: Bantam Books, 1992).

2. Benjamin Disraeli, *Alroy or The Prince of the Captivity,* in *The Works of Benjamin Disraeli, Earl of Beaconsfield, Embracing Novels, Romances, Plays, Poems, Biography, Short Stories and Great Speeches* (London: M. Walter Dunne, 1904), 20.

Epigraph: Stephen Bank, coauthor, with M. Kahn, of *The Sibling Bond.* (New York: Basic Books, 1982), xi.

1. C. G. Jung, *The Complete Works of C. G. Jung*, Gerhard Adler, ed., R. F. C. Hull, trans., vol. 7, *Two Essays on Analytical Psychology* (Princeton, NJ: Princeton University Press, 1967), para.109.

2. Nat Bennett, "Halfway or In-between or Something Else," in Elisa Albert, ed., *Freud's Blind Spot: 23 Original Essays on Cherished, Estranged, Lost, Hurtful, Hopeful, Complicated Siblings* (New York: Free Press, 2010), 251.

3. Kampan, *Ayodhya*, David Shulman, trans., Murty Classical Library of India (Cambridge, MA: Harvard University Press, in press), verse 791.

4. Mario Jacoby, *The Analytic Encounter* (Toronto: Inner City Books, 1984), 67.

5. Coleman, D., "Positive Sibling Transference: Theoretical and Clinical Dimensions," *Clinical Social Work Journal* 24:377–87.

6. Agger, E. M., "Psychoanalytic Perspectives on Sibling Relationships," *Psychoanalytic Inquiry* 8:3–30.

7. Deborah Blessing, "Hiding in Plain Sight: The Sibling Connection in Eating Disorders," *Journal of Child Psychotherapy* 33:36–50, and Jeanne Magagna, "Transformation: From Twin to Individual," *Journal of Child Psychotherapy* 33:51–69.

8. Sigmund. Freud, *The Letters of Sigmund Freud*, Ernest L. Freud, ed. (New York: Basic Books, 1960) 424, 483; "Letter to Fleiss, 3 October 1897," in Sigmund Freud, *The Complete Letters of Sigmund Freud to Wilhelm Fliess, 1887–1904*, Jeffrey Moussaieff Masson, ed. (Cambridge, MA: Belknap Press, 1986).

9. R. M. Lesser, "Sibling Transference and Counter-transference," *Journal of the American Academy of Psychoanalysis* 6:37–49.

10. Prophecy Coles, *The Importance of Sibling Relationships in Psychoanalysis* (London: Karnac Books, 2003), 9.

11. Marcy E. Stites, "Sibling Transference and Countertransference," 2005. Available at http://www.camft.org/ScriptContent/Professional_Ex/Articles/SiblingTransference.htm

12. Apparently "Cain complex" was first used in 1976, in Frances F. Schachter, Ellen Shore, Susan Feldman-Rotman, Ruth E. Marquis, and Susan Campbell, "Sibling Deidentification," *Developmental Psychology* 12 (5):418–27.

13. Murray Stein, "The Pattern of Envy and Sibling Rivalry in Myth and Religion." In *Psyche and Family: Jungian Applications to Family Therapy.* Edited

by L. Dodson and T. Gibson. (Wilmette, Illinois: Chiron Publications, 1996), 104.

14. Murray Stein, "The Pattern of Envy and Sibling Rivalry in Myth and Religion," 104.

15. Frances F. Schachter, "Sibling Deidentification in the Clinic: Devil vs. Angel," *Family Process* 24 (3):415–27.

16. Robert Jay Lifton, *The Broken Connection: On Death and the Continuity of Life* (New York: Simon & Schuster, 1979).

17. Henry Abramovitch, "Temenos Regained: Reflections on the Absence of the Analyst," *Journal of Analytical Psychology* 47:583–97, discusses a different aspect of Samuel's case.

18. Deborah Blessing, "Hiding in Plain Sight: The Sibling Connection in Eating Disorders," *Journal of Child Psychotherapy* 33:36–50.

Chapter 8

Epigraph: Nick Kelsh and Anna Quindlen, *Siblings* (New York: Studio, 1998), 110.

1. Author translation of Psalm 133:1.

2. http://www.brainyquote.com/quotes/authors/m/martin_luther_king_jr.htm

Bibliography

Abramovitch, Henry Hanoch (1992). "Disguise as a Transition to Homecoming." In *The Transcendent Function: Individual and Collective Aspects.* Edited by Mary Ann Matoon. Einsideln, Switzerland: Daimon Verlag.

———— (1994). *The First Father. Abraham: The Psychology and Culture of a Spiritual Revolutionary.* Lanham, MD: University Press of America. Reprint. Seattle, WA: Libertary, 2010.

———— (1997). "Temenos Lost: Reflections on Moving." *Journal of Analytical Psychology* 42:69–84.

———— (2002). "Temenos Regained: Reflections on the Absence of the Analyst." *Journal of Analytical Psychology* 47:583–97.

———— (2004). "Rabban Gamliel and Rabbi Yehoshua in the Analytic Training Institute: A Talmudic Text (Berachot 27b–28a) and the Group Life of Analysts." *Journal of Jungian Theory and Practice* 6 (2):21–40.

———— (2005). "The Neglect of Siblings in Depth Psychology." *San Francisco Jung Institute Library Journal* 23 (2):17–30.

Abt, Theodore (1988). *Progress without Loss of Soul.* Wilmette, IL: Chiron Publications.

Adams, Bert, N. (1968). *Kinship in an Urban Setting.* Chicago: Markham.

Adler, Alfred (1949). *Understanding Human Nature.* New York: Permabooks.

Agger, E. M. (1988). "Psychoanalytic Perspectives on Sibling Relationships." *Psychoanalytic Inquiry* 8:3–30.

Ainsfeld, Leon, and Arnold D. Richards (2000). *The Replacement Child: Variations on a Theme of History and Psychoanalysis.* Vol. 55 of *The Psychoanalytic Study of the Child.* New Haven, CT: Yale University Press.

Aksakoff, Sergei (1916). *Years of Childhood.* Translated by J. D. Duff. New York: Longmans, Green.

Albert, Elisa, ed. (2010). *Freud's Blind Spot: 23 Original Essays on Cherished, Estranged, Lost, Hurtful, Hopeful, Complicated Siblings.* New York: Free Press.

Ali, Ahmed, trans. (1988). Al-*Qur'an: A Contemporary Translation.* Princeton, NJ: Princeton University Press.

Alighieri, Dante (1997). *The Inferno of Dante: A New Verse Translation.* Translated by Robert Pinsky. London: Dent.

Alter, Robert (1981). *The Art of Biblical Narrative.* New York: Basic Books.

Alter, Robert, ed. (1996). *Genesis: Translation and Commentary*. New York: W. W. Norton.

American Psychiatric Association (2013), *Diagnostic and Statistical Manual of Mental Disorders,* 5th ed. Arlington, VA: American Psychiatric Association.

Aptowitzer, Viktor (1922*). Kain und Abel in der Agada, den Apokryphen, der hellenistichen, cristlichen und muhammedanischen Literatur.* Vienna: R. Lowitt Verlag.

Armstrong, Karen (1996). *In the Beginning: A New Interpretation of Genesis.* New York: Ballantine Books.

Ascher, Barbara Lazear (1992). *Landscape without Gravity: A Memoir of Grief.* Harrison, NY: Delphinium Books.

Auden, W. H., and Louis Kronenberger, eds. (1981). *The Viking Book of Aphorisms.* New York: Penguin Books.

Auerbach, Erich (1953). *Mimesis.* New York: Doubleday.

Axelrod, Richard. *The Evolution of Cooperation.* New York: Basic Books, 1984.

Axline, Virginia M. (1973). *Dibs: In Search of Self.* New York: Ballantine Books.

Aycock, D. Alan (1983). "The Mark of Cain." In *Structuralist Interpretations of Biblical Myth.* Edited by Edmund Leach and D. Alan Aycock. Cambridge: Cambridge University Press.

Bair, Deirdre (2004). *Jung: A Biography.* Boston, MA: Back Bay Books.

Bank, S., and M. Kahn (1982). *The Sibling Bond.* New York: Basic Books.

Barton, George A. (1920). *Archaeology and the Bible,* 3rd ed. Philadelphia: American Sunday School.

Baumrind, Diana (1973). "The Development of Instrumental Competence through Socialization." In *Minnesota Symposium on Child Psychology.* Edited by A. Pick. Minneapolis: University of Minnesota Press.

Beebe, John (1997). "The Case of Joan: A Classical Perspective." In *The Cambridge Companion to Jung.* Edited by Polly Young-Eisendrath and Terence Dawson. Cambridge: Cambridge University Press.

——— (1992). *Integrity in Depth.* College Station: Texas A&M University Press.

Benedek, Lisbeth von (2013*). Frére et Soeurs pour la Vie: L'Empreinte de la Fraterie sur nos Relations Adultes.* Paris: Eyrolles.

Berelson, B., and G. A. Steiner (1964). *Human Behavior: An Inventory of Scientific Findings.* New York: Harcourt, Brace & World.

Bixler, Ray H. (1982). "Sibling Incest in the Royal Families of Egypt, Peru and Hawaii." *Journal of Sex Research* 18:264–81.

Blanchard, R. (1997). "Birth Order and Sibling Sex Ratio in Homosexual versus Heterosexual Males and Females." *Annual Review of Sex Research* 8:27–67.

Blanchard, R., and A. F. Bogaert, "Homosexuality in Men and Number of Older Brothers," *American Journal of Psychiatry* 153:27–31.

Blessing, Deborah (2007). "Hiding in Plain Sight: The Sibling Connection in Eating Disorders." *Journal of Child Psychotherapy* 33:36–50.

Boer, Frits, and Judy Dunn (1992). *Children's Sibling Relationships: Developmental and Clinical Issues.* New York: Psychology Press.

Brammer-Savlov, Helen (2004). "Brother/Sister Archetype: Images of Contrasexual Sibling Bonds." Unpublished thesis, Independent Group of Analytical Psychologists, London.

Brams, Steven J. (1980). *Biblical Games: A Strategic Analysis of the Stories in the Old Testatment.* Cambridge, MA: MIT Press.

Brieger, Auguste (1934). *Kain und Abel in der deutschen Dichtung.* Berlin: de Gruyter.

Browning, Robert. *The Works of Robert Browning* (Ware, Herts: Wordsworth Editions, 1994).

Buber, Martin (1965). *The Knowledge of Man: A Philosophy of the Interhuman.* Edited by Maurice Friedman. New York: Harper Torchbooks.

Cain, A. C., and B. S. Cain (1964). "On Replacing a Child." *Journal of the American Academy of Child Psychiatry* 3:443–56.

Caffaro, John V., and Allison Conn-Caffaro (1998). *Sibling Abuse Trauma: Assessment and Intervention Strategies for Children, Families and Adults.* New York: Haworth Press.

Cassuto, Umberto (1964). *A Commentary on the Book of Genesis. Parts 1 and 2.* Translated by I. Abrahams. Jerusalem: Magnes Press.

Chodorow, Joan (1997). *Jung on Active Imagination.* Princeton, NJ: Princeton Univesity Press.

Cicirelli, Victor (1989). "Feelings of Attachment to Siblings and Well-being in Later Life." *Psychology and Aging* 4:211–16.

———— (1995). *Sibling Relationships across the Lifespan.* New York: Plenum Press.

Clark, Taylor (2008). "Plight of the Little Emperors." *Psychology Today.* http://www.psychologytoday.com/articles/200806/plight-the-little-emperors

Cocteau, Jean (1930). *Enfants Terrible.* Translated by Samuel Putnam. New York: Brewer & Warren.

Cohen, A. A., and P. Mendes-Flohr, eds. (1987). *Contemporary Jewish Religious Thought: Original Essays on Critical Concepts, Movements and Beliefs.* New York: Scribners.

Coleman, D. (1996). "Positive Sibling Transference: Theoretical and Clinical Dimensions." *Clinical Social Work Journal* 24:377–87.

Coles, Prophecy (2003). *The Importance of Sibling Relationships in Psychoanalysis.* London: Karnac Books.

———, ed. (2006). *Sibling Relationships.* London: Karnac Books.

Colona, Alice B., and Lottie M. Newman (1983). "Psychoanalytic Literature on Siblings." *The Psychoanalytic Study of the Child* 38:285–309.

Coltart, N. (1991). "The Silent Patient." *Psychoanalytic Dialogues* 1:439–53.

Combs, Eugene (1988). "Has Yhwh Cursed the Ground? Perplexity of Interpretation in Genesis 1–5." In *Ascribe to the Lord: Biblical and Other Studies in Memory of Peter C. Craigie.* Edited by Lyle Eslinger and GlenTaylor. JSOT Supplement Series No. 67. Sheffield: Sheffield Academic Press.

Cooper, Howard (1987). "Persecution and Silence: The Myth of Cain and Abel." *Harvest* 33:7–27.

Dahlberg, Bruce T. (1982). "The Unity of Genesis." In *Literary Interpretations of Biblical Narratives.* Vol.2, pp. 126–34. Edited by K. Gros Louis. Nashville: Abingdon.

Dali, Salvador (1942). *The Secret Life of Salvador Dali.* New York: Dial Press.

Dershowitz, Alan M. (2000). *The Genesis of Justice: Ten Stories of Biblical Injustice That Led to the Ten Commandments and Modern Law.* New York: Warner Books.

De Tiva-Raeburn, Elizabeth (2004). *The Empty Room.* New York: Scribners'.

Disraeli, Benjamin. *Alroy or The Prince of the Captivity.* In *The Works of Benjamin Disraeli, Earl of Beaconsfield, Embracing Novels, Romances, Plays, Poems, Biography, Short Stories and Great Speeches.* London: M. Walter Dunne, 1904.

Dorris, Michael (1996). "The Story of Abel." In *Genesis as It Is Written: Contemporary Writers on Our First Stories.* Edited by David Rosenberg. San Francisco: Harper.

Downing, Christine (2007). *Psyche's Sisters: Re-Imagining the Meaning of Sisterhood.* Dallas, TX: Spring Journal.

Dunn, J. (2001). "Psychology of Sibling Relations." In *International Encyclopedia of the Social and Behavioral Sciences,* 14036–66. Edited by N. J. Smelser and Paul B. Baltes. Oxford: Pergamon.

——— (1985). *Sisters and Brothers: The Developing Child.* Cambridge, MA: Harvard University Press.

Dunn, J., and C. Kendrick (1982). *Siblings: Love, Envy and Understanding.* Cambridge, MA: Harvard University Press.

Dunn, J., C. Kendrick, and R. MacNamee (1981). "The Reaction of First-born Children to the Birth of a Sibling: Mothers' Reports." *Journal of Child Psychology and Psychiatry* 22:1–18.

Dunn, J., and P. Munn (1987) "Development of Justifications in Disputes with Mother and Children." *Developmental Psychology* 23:791–98.

Dunn, J., and R. Plomin (1990). *Separate Lives: Why Siblings Are So Different.* New York: Basic Books.

Edinger, Edward F. (1986) *The Bible and the Psyche: Individuation Symbolism in the Old Testament.* Toronto: Inner City Books.

——— (1973). *Ego and Archetype: Individuation and the Religious Function of the Psyche.* Boston, MA: Shambhala Publications.

Edward, Joyce (2012). *The Sibling Relationship: A Force for Growth and Conflict.* Northvale, NJ: Jason Aaronson.

Edwards, O. D. (1992). "Druids, Priests, Bards, and Other Fathers." In *Fatherhood: Men Writing about Fathering.* Edited by S. French. London: Virago.

Eichhorn, David Max (1957). *Cain: The Son of the Serpent.* Chappaqua, NY: Rossel Books.

Eissler, Ruth S., Albert J. Solnit, and Peter B. Neubauer, eds. (1983). *The Psychoanalytic Study of the Child.* Vol. 38. New Haven, CT: Yale University Press.

Ellis, Joseph J. (2000). *Founding Brothers: The Revolutionary Generation.* New York: Vintage Books.

Engel, George (1975). "The Death of a Twin." *International Journal of Psychoanalysis* 56:23–40.

Ernst, Cecile, and Jules Angst (1983) *Birth Order: Its Influence on Personality.* Berlin: Springer-Verlag.

Even-Shoshan, Avraham (1989). *A New Concordance of the Old Testament: Thesaurus of the Language of the Bible Hebrew and Aramaic Roots, Words, Proper Names, Phrases and Synonyms.* Ada, MI: Baker Publishing Group.

Exley, Helen, ed. (1996). *Brothers! Quotations Selected by Helen Exley.* New York: Helen Exley Giftbooks.

——— (2009). *Sisters! A Little Gift Book.* New York: Helen Exley Giftbooks.

Fairbairn, W. R. D. (1981). *Psychoanalytic Studies of Personality: The Object Relation Theory of Personality.* London: Routledge & Kegan Paul.

Fanos, J. H., and B. G. Nickerson (1991). "Long Term Effects of Sibling Death during Adolescence." *Journal of Adolescent Research* 6:70–82.

Felson, R. B. (1983). "Aggression and Violence between Siblings." *Social Psychology Quarterly* 46:271–85.

Felson R. B., and N. Russo (1988). "Parental Punishment and Sibling Aggression." *Social Psychology Quarterly* 51:11–18.

Fishbane, Michael (1979). *Text and Texture: Close Readings of Selected Biblical Texts.* New York: Schocken Books.

Flomenhoft, D. (2006). "The Forgotten Ones: The Grief Experience of Adult Siblings of WTC Victims." Ph.D. dissertation. New York University. In Joyce Edward (2012). *The Sibling Relationship.*

Fordham, Frida (1966). *An Introduction to Jung's Psychology.* 3rd ed. Baltimore: Penguin.

Forsyth, Dan W. (1991). "Sibling Rivalry, Aesthetic Sensibility and Social Structures in Genesis." *Ethos* 19:453–510.

Fortes, Meyer (1974). "The First Born." *Journal of Child Psychology and Psychiatry* 15:81–104.

Fox, Everett, trans. (1995) *The Five Books of Moses.* New York: Schocken Books.

Freedman, H., and Maurice Simon, trans. (1939). *Midrash Rabbah.* 10 Vols. London: Soncino Press.

Sigmund Freud (1918). *The Standard Edition of the Complete Psychological Works of Sigmund Freud.* Vol. 17. *An Infantile Neurosis and Other Works.* London: The Hogarth Press and the Institute of Psycho-analysis.

Freud, Sigmund (1958). *The Interpretation of Dreams.* Vols. 4 and 5. Translated by James Strachey. London: Hogarth Press. First published in 1900–1901 as vols. 4 and 5 in *The Standard Edition of the Complete Psychological Works of Sigmund Freud.* Edited by James Strachey. London: Hogarth Press and the Institute of Psycho-Analysis.

——— (1966). *Introductory Lectures on Psychoanalysis.* Translated by James Strachey. New York: Norton. First published in 1915–16 as vol. 15 in *The Standard Edition of the Complete Psychological Works of Sigmund Freud.* Edited by James Strachey. London: The Hogarth Press and the Institute of Psycho-analysis.

Fuller, Victoria G., and Catherine Crowther (1998). "A Dark Talent: Silence in Analysis." *Journal of Analytical Psychology* 43:523–43.

Gilligan, Carol (1982). *In a Different Voice: Psychological Theory and Women's Development.* Cambridge, MA: Harvard University Press.

Gilligan, James (1994). *Violence: Our Deadly Epidemic and Its Causes.* New York: Putnam's Sons.

Ginzberg, Louis (1969). *The Legends of the Jews.* 7 vols. Philadelphia, PA: The Jewish Publication Society.

Gold, Deborah, T. (1989). "Sibling Relations in Old Age: A Typology." *International Journal of Aging and Human Development* 28:37–51.

Graves, Robert and Patai, Raphael (1963). *Hebrew Myths: The Book of Genesis.* London: Cassell.

Greenspahn, Frederick E. (1994). *When Brothers Dwell Together: The Preeminence of Younger Siblings in the Hebrew Bible.* New York: Oxford University Press.

Gros Louis, K., ed. (1982). *Literary Interpretations of Biblical Narratives.* Vol. 2. Nashville, TN: Abingdon.

Grosskurth, P. (1985) *Melanie Klein: Her Work and Her World*. London: Maresfield Library.

Hammer, Reuven (1995). *The Classsic Midrash: Tannaitic Commentaries on the Bible*. Mahwah, NJ: Paulist Press.

Hansen, Ron (1996). "The Story of Cain." In *Genesis as It Is Written: Contemporary Writers on Our First Stories*. Edited by David Rosenberg. San Francisco: Harper

Harris, Irving (1964). *The Promised Seed: A Comparative Study of First and Later Sons*. New York: Free Press.

Hartman, Geoffrey, and Sanford Budick, eds. (1986). Midrash and Literature. New Haven, CT: Yale University Press.

Heller, Joseph (1984). *God Knows*. New York: Alfred A. Knopf.

Hepburn, Katharine (1991) *Me: Stories of My Life*. London: Penguin.

Hetherington, E. Mavis (1988). "Parents, Children and Siblings: Six Years After." In *Relations within Families*. Edited by R. A. Hinde and J. Stevenson-Hinde. Oxford: Oxford University Press.

Herion, Gary A. (1995). "Why God Rejected Cain's Offering: The Obvious Answer." In *Fortunate the Eyes That See: Essays in Honor of David Noel Freeman in Celebration of His Seventieth Birthday*. Edited by Astrid B. Beck, Andrew H. Bartlett, Paul R. Raabe, and Chris A. Franke. Grand Rapids, MI: Eerdmans.

Hilgard, Josephine R. (1951). "Sibling Rivalry and Social Heredity." *Psychiatry* 14:375–85.

Horowitz, Donald L. *The Deadly Ethnic Riot*. Berkeley: University of California Press, 2001.

Hua, Cai (2001). *A Society without Fathers or Husbands*. New York: Zone.

Ignatieff, M. (2001). "The Danger of a World without Enemies: Lemkin's Word." *The New Republic Online:* http://www.thenewrepublic.com/022601/ignatieff022601.html

———— (1998). *The Warrior's Honor: Ethnic War and the Modern Conscience*. New York: Metropolitan Books.

Jacobson, Harold (1992). *The Very Model of a Man*, New York: Viking,

Jacoby, Mario (1984). *The Analytic Encounter*. Toronto: Inner City Books.

Jerusalem Bible, Readers Edition (1966). Edited by Alexander Jones. Garden City, NY: Doubleday.

Jones, Ernest (1953). *Sigmund Freud: A Life and Work*. Vol. 1. London: Hogarth Press.

Joubert, Dereck, and Beverly Joubert (1992). *Natural Enemies: Lions and Hyenas*. National Geographic Video.

Jung, C. G. (1970). "Answer to Job." Pages 359–470 in *Psychology and Religion: West and East.* Vol. 11 in *The Collected Works of C. G. Jung.* Edited by Gerhard Adler. Translated by R. F. C. Hull. Princeton, NJ: Princeton University Press.

———— (1969). *Aion: Researches into the Phenomenology of the Self.* Vol. 9. Part 2 in *The Collected Works of C. G. Jung.* Edited by Gerhard Adler. Translated by R. F. C. Hull. Princeton, NJ: Princeton University Press.

———— (1954–90). *The Collected Works of C. G. Jung.* 21 vols. Edited by Gerhard Adler. Translated by R. F. C. Hull. Princeton, NJ: Princeton University Press.

———— (1969). *The Psychology of the Transference.* Princeton, NJ: Princeton University Press.

———— (2009). *The Red Book.* Edited by Sonu Shamdasami. Translated by Sonu Shamdasani, Mark Kyburz, and John Peck. New York: W. W. Norton.

Jung, Carl, and Aniela Jaffé (1963). *Memories, Dreams, Reflections.* London: Collins.

Kahn, M. D., and K. G. Lewis (1988). *Siblings in Therapy: Life Span and Clinical Issues.* New York: Norton.

Kalish, Richard A. (1985). *Death, Grief, and Caring Relationships.* Monterey, CA: Brooks/Cole.

Kampan (in press). *Ayodhya.* Translated by David Shulman. Murty Classical Library of India. Cambridge, MA: Harvard University Press.

Kaplan, H. I., and B. J. Sadock (1997). *Concise Textbook of Clinical Psychiatry.* Baltimore, MD: Williams & Wilkins.

Kast, Verena (1986). *Brother Husband and Sister Wife.* Wilmette, IL: Chiron Publications.

Kelsh, Nick, and Anna Quindlen (1998). *Siblings.* New York: Penguin Studio.

Kepnes, Steven (2009). "Hagar and Esau: From Others to Sisters and Brothers." Pages 31–46 in *Crisis, Call, and Leadership in the Abrahamic Traditions.* Edited by Peter Ochs and William Stacy Johnson. New York: Palgrave Macmillan).

Keynes, Randal (2001). *Darwin, His Daughter, and Human Evolution.* New York: Riverhead Books.

Khan, Masud (1963). "Silence as Communication." In *Privacy of the Self.* London: International Psychology Library.

Kiell, Norman, ed. (1983) *Blood Brothers: Siblings as Writers.* New York: International Universities Press.

Kincaid, Jamaica (1998). *My Brother.* New York: Farrar, Straus and Giroux.

Klagsburn, Francine (1992). *Mixed Feelings: Love, Hate, Rivalry, and Reconciliation among Brothers and Sisters.* New York: Bantam Books.

Klein, Melanie (1975). *Love, Guilt, and Reparation and Other Works 1921–1945.* Vol. 1 in *The Collected Writings of Melanie Klein.* Edited by Roger Money-Kyrle. London: Hogarth Press.

———— (1975). *Narrative of a Child Analysis: The Conduct of the Psycho-Analysis of Children as Seen in the Treatment of a Ten-Year-Old Boy. Vol. 4 in The Writings of Melanie Klein.* London: Hogarth Press.

———— (1975). *The Psychoanalysis of Children.* Vol. 2 in The Collected Writings of Melanie Klein. Edited by Roger Money-Kyrle. London: Hogarth Press.

Kriegal, Leonard (1999). *Flying Solo: Reimagining Manhood, Courage, and Loss.* Boston, MA: Beacon Press.

Kugel, J. L. (1994). "Hatred and Revenge." Pages 214–46 in *In Potiphar's House: The Interpretive Life of Biblical Texts.* Cambridge, MA: Harvard University Press.

Lafser. M. (2002). *Longing for My Child: Reflections for Parents and Siblings after a Child's Death.* Loyola University Press.

Lal, P. (1970). *Mahabharata of Vyasa.* Glen Oaks, NY: Asia Book Company of America.

Lamb, M. E., and B. Sutton-Smith, eds. (1982). *Sibling Relationships: Their Nature and Significance across the Lifespan.* Hillsdale, NJ: Erlbaum.

Lao Tsu (1989). *Tao Te Ching: A New English Version.* Translated by Stephen A. Mitchell. New York: HarperCollins.

Leach, Edmund (1983). "Why Did Moses Have a Sister?" In *Structuralist Interpretations of Biblical Myth.* Edited by Edmund Leach and D. Alan Aycock. Cambridge: Cambridge University Press.

Leder, J. M. (1991). *Brothers and Sisters: How They Shape Our Lives.* With a foreword by S. Bank. New York: Ballantine.

Lesser, R. M. (1978). "Sibling Transference and Counter-transference." *Journal of the American Academy of Psychoanalysis* 6:37–49.

Levinson, Daniel J., Charlotte N. Darrow, and Edward B. Klein (1978). *The Seasons of a Man's Life.* New York: Ballantine.

Levy, David (1937). *Studies in Sibling Rivalry.* New York: American Orthopsychiatric Association.

Lewis, Helen Block (1976). *Psychic War in Men and Women.* New York: New York University Press.

Licht, Jacob (1986). *Storytelling in the Bible.* Jerusalem: Magnes Press.

Lichtheim, Miriam (1976). *Ancient Egyptian Literature.* Vol. 2. *The New Kingdom.* Berkeley: University of California Press.

Lifton, Robert Jay (1979). *The Broken Connection: On Death and the Continuity of Life.* New York: Simon & Schuster.

Lindholm, Charles (1982). *Generosity and Jealousy: The Swat Pukhtun of Northen Pakistan.* New York: Columbia University Press.

McNaron, T. A. H. (1985). *The Sister Bond: A Feminist View of a Timeless Connection.* New York: Pergamon Press.

Magagna, Jeanne (2007). "Transformation: From Twin to Individual." *Journal of Child Psychotherapy* 33:51–69.

Márai, Sándor (2002). *Embers.* Translated by Carol Brown Janeway. New York: Vintage.

Marcus, Clare Cooper (1997). *House as a Mirror of Self: Exploring the Deeper Meaning of Home.* Berkeley, CA: Conari Press.

Marshall, M., ed. (1979). *Siblingship in Oceania: Studies in the Meaning of Kin Relations.* Lanham, MD: University Press of America.

Martell, Yann (2002). *The Life of Pi.* New York: Houghton Mifflin Harcourt.

Mellinkoff, Ruth (1981). *The Mark of Cain.* Berkeley: University of California Press.

Midrash Rabbah (1939). Translated by H. Freedman and Maurice Simon. Vols. 1–3. *Genesis.* London: Soncino Press.

Miller, Arthur (1996). "The Story of Adam and Eve." In *Genesis as It Is Written: Contemporary Writers on Our First Stories.* Edited by David Rosenberg. San Francisco: Harper

Mitchell, Juliet (2004). *Siblings: Sex and Violence.* London: Polity Press.

Mock, Douglas W., and Geoffrey A. Parker (1997). *The Evolution of Sibling Rivalry.* Oxford: Oxford University Press.

Moore, Thomas (1995). *Care of the Soul.* London: Piatkus.

Muhawi, Ibrahim, and Sharif Kanaana. *Speak, Bird, Speak Again: Palestinian Arab Folktales.* Berkeley: University of California Press, 1989.

Neusner, Jacob (1994). *The Midrash: An Introduction.* Northvale, NJ: Jason Aronson.

Newton, Lara (2007). *Brothers and Sisters: Discovering the Psychology of Companionship.* Dallas: Spring Journal.

Nuckolls, Charles W., ed. (1993). *Siblings in South Asia: Brothers and Sisters in Cultural Context.* New York: Guilford Press.

Ochs, Peter, and William Stacy Johnson, eds. (2009). *Crisis, Call, and Leadership in the Abrahamic Traditions.* New York: Palgrave Macmillan.

Ogden, T. H. (1992). "The Dialectically Constituted/Decentered Subject of Psychoanalysis 2: The Contributions of Klein and Winnicott." *International Journal of Psychoanalysis* 73:613–26.

——— (1989). *The Primitive Edge of Experience.* Northvale, NJ: Jason Aronson.

Pagis, Dan (1989). *The Selected Poetry of Dan Pagis.* Translated by Stephen Mitchell. Berkeley: University of California Press.

Paine, Robert (1999). "'Am I My Brother's Keeper?' (Genesis 4:9): Violence and the Making of Society." *Qualitative Sociology* 24:169–89.

Patterson, G. R. (1984). "Siblings: Fellow Travelers in Coercive Family Processes." Pages 173–215 in *Advances in the Study of Aggression.*

Edited by R. J. Blanchard and D. C. Blanchard. Orlando, FL: Academic Press.

Paul, Robert A. (1996). *Moses and Civilization: The Meaning behind Freud's Myth.* New Haven, CT: Yale University Press.

Plomin, Robert, and Denise Daniels (1987). "Why Are Children in the Same Family So Different from One Another?' *Behavioral and Brain Sciences* 10:1–60.

Pritchard, J. B., ed. (1969). *Ancient Near Eastern Texts Relating to the Old Testament.* 3rd ed. Princeton, NJ: Princeton University Press.

Porot M. (1993). *L'Enfant de remplacement,* Paris: Frison-Roche.

Quinones, Ricardo J. (1991). *The Changes of Cain: Violence and the Lost Brother in the Cain and Abel Literature.* Princeton, NJ: Princeton University Press.

Rapoport, Anatol (1999). *Two-Person Game Theory.* Mineola, NY: Dover.

Ravitsky, Ruth (2001). *Korot Bereshit: Creative Women Write about the Book of Genesis.* Tel Aviv: Yediot Akharonot (Hebrew).

Rosen, H., and H. L. Cohen (1981). "Children's Reactions to Sibling Loss." *Clinical Social Work Journal* 9:211–19.

Rustin, Margaret (2007). "Taking Account of Siblings: A View from Child Psychotherapy" *Journal of Child Psychotherapy* 33:21–35.

Samuels, Andrew (1985). *Jung and the Post-Jungians.* London: Routledge & Kegan Paul.

Sandmaier, M. (1994). *Original Kin.* New York: Dutton.

Santiago, L. (1973). *The Children of Oedipus: Brother-Sister Incest in Psychiatry, Literature, History and Mythology.* Roslyn Heights, NY: Libra.

Sarna, Nahum M. (1966). *Understanding Genesis.* New York: Jewish Theological Seminary with McGraw-Hill.

Schachter, Frances F. (1985). "Sibling Deidentification in the Clinic: Devil vs. Angel." *Family Process* 24 (3):415–27.

Schachter, Frances F., Ellen Shore, Susan Feldman-Rotman, Ruth E. Marquis, and Susan Campbell (1976). "Sibling Deidentification." *Developmental Psychology* 12 (5):418–27.

Schachter F. F., and R. K. Stone, eds. (1987). *Practical Concerns about Siblings: Bridging the Research-Practice Gap.* New York: Haworth Press.

Schapera, I. (1955). "The Sin of Cain." *Journal of the Royal Anthropological Institute of Great Britain and Northern Ireland* 85:33–43.

Schellinski, Kristina (2006). "Life after Death: The Replacement Child's Search for Self." In *Barcelona 2004: Edges of Experience: Memory and Emergence. Proceedings of the 16th Annual International IAAP Congress for Analytical Psychology.* Edited by Lyn Cowan. Einsiedeln, Switzer-

land: Daimon Verlag. http://www.iaap.org/index.php?option=com_
content&view=article&id=530:life-after-death-the-replacement-childs-
search-for-self&catid=567:tuesday-august-31-2004&Itemid=508

———— (2002). "'Oh, Brother:' A Jungian Perspective on the Challenges and
Opportunities Faced by a Replacement Child." Diploma Thesis. C.G. Jung
Institute, Zurich.

———— (2012). "Replacement Child." Presentation at the 2nd European Conference on Analytical Psychology, St. Petersburg, 31 August.

———— (2014). "Who am I?" *Journal of Analytical Psychology* 59:189–211.

Schwartz, Regina M. (1997). *The Curse of Cain: The Violent Legacy of Monothe-
ism*. Chicago: University of Chicago Press.

Segal, Nancy, L. (1999). *Entwined Lives: Twins and What They Tell Us about Human Behavior*. New York: Dutton.

Sharpe, S. A., and A. D. Rosenblatt (1994). "Oedipal Sibling Triangles." *Journal of
American Psychoanalysis Association* 42:491–523.

Sharon, Diane M. (2001). "Rivalry in Genesis: A New Reading." *Conservative
Judiasm* 53:19–35.

Sprinzak, Ehud (1999). *Brother against Brother: Violence and Extremism in
Israeli Politics* from *Altalena* to the Rabin Assassination. New York: Free
Press.

Stein, Murray (1996). "The Pattern of Envy and Sibling Rivalry in Myth
and Religion." In *Psyche and Family: Jungian Applications to Family
Therapy*. Edited by L. Dodson and T. Gibson. Wilmette, IL: Chiron
Publications.

Straight Story, The (1999). Directed by David Lynch. Disney Studios.

Straus, Murray A., and Richard J. Gelles (1986). "Societal Change and Change in
Family Violence from 1975 to 1985 as Revealed by Two National Surveys."
Journal of Marriage and Family 48 (3):465–79.

Suitor, J. Jill, Jori Sechrist, and Karl Pillemer (2007). "When Mothers Have Favorites: Conditions under Which Mothers Differentiate among Their Adult
Children." *Canadian Journal on Aging* 26:85–99.

Sullivan, Harry Stack (1968). *Theory of Interpersonal Relation*. New York: Norton.

Sullivan, Louis (1992). *Changemakers: A Jungian Perspective on Sibling Position
and Family Atmosphere*. London: Routledge & Kegan Paul.

Sulloway, Frank J. (1996). *Born to Rebel: Birth Order, Family Dynamics, and
Creative Lives*. New York: Pantheon Books.

———— (2001). "Sibling-Order Effects." In *International Encyclopedia of the
Social and Behavioral Sciences*. Edited by N. J. Smelser and Paul B. Baltes.
Pergamon, Oxford, 14058–63.

Sutton-Smith, Brian, and B. G. Rosenberg (1970). *The Sibling.* New York: Holt, Rinehart & Winston.

Syrén, Roger (1993). "The Forsaken First-Born: A Study of a Recurrent Motif in the Patriarchal Narratives." *Journal for the Study of the Old Testament: Supplement Series* 133.

Tammuz, Benjamin (1999). "My Brother." In *Six Israeli Novellas.* Edited by Gershon Shaked. Boston: David R. Godine, 212–303.

Treffers, Philip D. A. (1992). "Foreword: Sibling Studies and Sibling Lore." In *Children's Sibling Relationships: Developmental and Clinical Issues.* Edited by Frits Boer and Judy Dunn. London: Psychology Press.

Toman, Walter (1992). *Family Constellation: Its Effect on Personality and Social Behavior.* 4th ed. New York: Springer-Verlag.

Unamuno, Miguel de (1954). *Tragic Sense of Life.* New York: Dover.

Umberton, Debra (2006). *Death of a Parent: Transition to a New Adult Identity.* Cambridge: Cambridge University Press.

Vaillant, George E., and Caroline O. Vaillant (1990). "Natural History of Male Psychological Health, 12: A Forty-Five-Year Study of the Predictors of Successful Aging at Age Sixty-Five." *American Journal of Psychiatry* 147:31–37.

Van Frantz, Marie-Louise (1999). *Puer Aeternis.* Toronto: Inner City Books.

Visotzsky, Burton, L. (1996). *The Ethics of Genesis: How the Tormented Family of Genesis Leads Us to Moral Development.* New York: Crown Publishers.

Vitz, P. C. (1988). *Sigmund Freud's Christian Unconscious.* New York: Guilford Press.

Volkan, Vamik D., and Gabriele Ast (1997). *Siblings in the Unconscious and Psychopathology: Womb Fantasies, Claustrophobias, Fear of Pregnancy, Murderous Rage, Animal Symbolism, Christmas and Easter "Neuroses," and Twinnings or Identifications with Sisters and Brothers.* Madison, CT: International Universities Press.

Walzer, Michael, "The Triumph of Just War Theory (and the Dangers of Success)." *Social Research* 69 (4): 925–44.

Weinfeld, M., ed. (1993). *The World of the Bible: Genesis.* Tel Aviv, Israel: Davidson-Eti (Hebrew).

Westermann, Claus (1984). *Genesis 1–11: A Commentary.* Translated by J. J. Scullion. Minneapolis: Augsburg Publishing.

Wiehe, V. (1990). *Sibling Abuse: Hidden Physical, Emotional and Sexual Trauma.* New York: Lexington Press.

Wierzbicka, Anna (1997). *Understanding Cultures through Their Key Words: English, Russian, Polish, German, and Japanese.* Oxford: Oxford University Press.

Winnicott, D. W. (1978). *The Piggle: An Account of the Psychoanalytic Treatment of a Little Girl,* London, Hogarth Press.

"Wolfman, the," pseud. (1973). "Recollections of My Childhood." In *The Wolfman and Sigmund Freud.* Edited by M. Gardiner. New York: Penguin Books, 17–133.

Zagajewski, Adam (1995). *Two Cities: On Exile, History and the Imagination.* New York: Farrar, Straus, Giroux.

Zion, Noam (1990). *On The Origins of Human Violence. An Introduction to Midrash Agada: The Story of Cain and Abel.* 2 vols. Jerusalem: Shalom Hartman Institute (Hebrew).

Zoja, Luigi (2001). *The Father.* London: Routledge.

Zornberg, Aviva Gottlieb (1995). *The Beginning of Desire: Reflections on Genesis.* New York: Schocken Books.

Zukov, P. (1989). *Sibling Interaction across Cultures: Theoretical and Methodological Issues.* New York: Springer-Verlag.